THE PERSISTENCE OF SOCIAL INEQUALITY IN AMERICA

THE PERSISTENCE OF
SOCIAL INEQUALITY
IN AMERICA

BY
JOHN DALPHIN

Copyright © 1981

Schenkman Publishing Company Inc.
3 Mount Auburn Place
Cambridge, Massachusetts 02138

Library of Congress Cataloging in Publication Data

Dalphin, John,
  The persistence of social inequality in
America
  Bibliography: p. 139
  1. Social classes—United States. 2. Equality.
I. Title.
HN90.S6D34   305.5'0973   81-4561
ISBN 0-87073-614-0   AACR2
ISBN 0-87073-615-9 (pbk.)

PRINTED IN THE UNITED STATES OF AMERICA

CONTENTS

PREFACE

The reading material for courses in social stratification and social inequality generally can be classified into one of the following two areas: 1) texts that attempt to present all major theory and research on social stratification and social inequality—a good example is *The Structure of Social Inequality* by Vanfossen; or 2) paperbacks that give an in-depth analysis of a specific part of the stratification system—such as *The Hidden Injuries of Class* by Sennet and Cobb which deals with the blue-collar world. The professor ordering books for his or her course often faces a dilemma: Should a text be ordered that gives a general overview of social stratification and social inequality? Or, should a number of more interesting paperbacks be used, sacrificing the unifying perspective of a single text? The expense of books today often eliminates the possibility of following both directions. *The Persistence of Social Inequality in America* aims to give a unifying perspective typical of the better core textbooks, and yet its size and tone will allow it to be used with a number of additional paperbacks.

The present book organizes key stratification issues and findings around some central questions of interest to the reader: Why do stratification and inequality persist in America? How do Americans perceive the nature of the stratification system? How and why are income, wealth, and power concentrated in the hands of the upper class? What prevents non-upper class Americans from demanding and achieving change in the distribution of income, wealth, and power? It is hoped that the provocative themes of the book will make it suitable not only in social stratification and social inequality courses, but also as supplementary reading in related courses (introductory sociology, political sociology, social change, and social problems) and as compelling reading for the general population.

ACKNOWLEDGEMENTS

A number of people have been very helpful to me in the process of writing this book. John Murray made many important substantive and editorial suggestions. John Fleming gave considerable editorial assistance. David Eisenhower, William Frain, Gerald Matross, Maynard Seider, and John Williamson provided helpful comments on various drafts of the manuscript. The Faculty Development Committee at Merrimack College awarded me grants which allowed me to have the time and resources necessary for completion of the book. Finally, family and friends were very supportive of me. To all of the above, go my sincere thanks.

CLASS AND STATUS STRATIFICATION

J. Paul Getty, the oil magnate, had an estimated *daily* income of $300,000. Assuming a normal working day, this means that he earned $75,000 by the time doughnuts arrived for his morning coffee break. Less than one percent of all American families have a *yearly* income of $75,000. In fact, the yearly income for "middle Americans" is less than $20,000, an income level at which families have to struggle to make ends meet. What must life be like, then, for the fourteen percent of American families who are at or below the poverty level? That a large percentage of dog food in America is consumed not by dogs but rather by people is only one example of survival strategies developed by the poor.

What allows such gross economic disparities to exist? What prevents those who are not part of the upper class from demanding and achieving change in the distribution of income, wealth, and power? Why does social inequality persist in America? Although much work has been done by social scientists in the areas of social inequality and social stratification, these questions have been relatively unattended in recent years. Consequently, this book addresses these central questions.

FUNDAMENTAL CONCEPTS

In order to set the stage for a discussion of the concentration of income, wealth, and power in America, it is necessary to introduce briefly some basic terminology. The concepts of social inequality, stratification, social class, and social status are pivotal.

Underlying all discussions in this area is the concept of

social inequality. Although social scientists generally do not offer a formal definition for inequality, they assume that the term implies some degree of social or economic disparity. Many different forms of social inequality exist in American society: racial inequality, sexual inequality, inequality as a result of age differences, and others. The inequalities to which blacks, women, and the elderly have been exposed are well documented; but the most basic form of inequality in America, and perhaps in all societies, is what social scientists refer to as stratification. **Social stratification** suggests that a society has divisions, cleavages, or splits within it. More specifically, it means that a society is divided into hierarchically arranged levels of families (and, increasingly, individuals), who have unequal access to what is valued in that society.

Sociologists often refer to these hierarchically arranged levels of families or individuals into which society is stratified as **social classes**. They are broadly defined as groups of families or individuals with similar amounts of income, wealth, prestige, and political power. The use of the term social class in this book is more restrictive and will reflect the more traditional understanding of social class found in the works of Karl Marx and Max Weber. Both suggest that a social class is made up of families and individuals who have a similar economic position, determined by their property, wealth, and source of income. Social class position is not defined by level of prestige or political power according to this interpretation of social class.

Most societies are stratified to a considerable degree along social-class (eonomic) lines. The initial comments on the income distribution in America provide a good example. But it is important to note that a society also can be stratified according to **social status**, which is defined as the prestige granted to familes or individuals on the basis of who or what they are. As such, status reflects the degree of recognition and acceptance that a family or individual experiences in a particular society. Determinants of status vary from society to society; but the most common ones are occupation, education, and family lineage. Most societies have a significant amount of stratification on the basis of social status. For example, in American society white-collar workers as a group are accorded higher status than are blue-collar workers.

A final point to consider is that class stratification and status stratification can sometimes be independent of one another. An individual, for example, can have high-class (economic) position and relatively low-status (prestige) position—as would a member of organized crime. Or, a person can have relatively high status (prestige) position and low class (economic position)— for example, a teacher. This chapter will later elaborate upon the relationship between class stratification and status stratification.

POPULAR IMAGES OF SOCIAL INEQUALITY

Before considering the actual research done by sociologists on the American stratification system, it is worthwhile to briefly examine laymen's views of social inequality.

Leonard Reissman (1973) has made an interesting observation: the Cornell University library has fifteen times as many references to equality as it does to inequality. He argues that this shows the desire of Americans to focus their attention upon the positive goal of equality rather than upon the negative reality of inequality.

While the major thrust of what Reissman is saying can be agreed with, his comments should be amended by saying that even with respect to the objective of equality there is considerable ambiguity on the part of Americans. What kind of equality is supported: equality of opportunity or equality of condition? The latter, which represents true equality among people is difficult for most of us to imagine. If asked to describe the images that come to mind when they think of a society with true equality (equality of condition), most people would draw a blank. This is because we live in a society where social inequality and stratification are taken for granted as parts of the natural order of things. The Orwellian maxim, "All animals are equal, but some animals are more equal than others," has become internalized by most Americans.

The kind of equality valued by Americans is equality of opportunity, not equality of condition. This means that everyone should have an equal chance to make something of himself or herself, a crucial part of the American Dream Package. The

Package also includes an emphasis on individualism, competition, the work ethic, social mobility, and success—look out for yourself, be competitive, and work hard. Because equal opportunity exists, so the Dream goes, the individual who behaves appropriately will be socially mobile and successful: Horatio Alger heroes have made it, and so can you.

When the realities of inequality become recognized by Americans, they take refuge in the belief that those at the bottom can improve their situation if they work hard and strive to get ahead. The American Dream Package is there for those at the bottom of society, too, if they only will unwrap it. This theme dominates much of the media. One of the most popular movies in recent years, is an example. In *Rocky,* the hero (The Italian Stallion) makes a meteoric rise from a down-and-out, washed-up fighter to championship challenger overnight. Audiences often stand and applaud at the end of the film because, one suspects, they are pleased to see their own fantasies of social mobility and success come to life on the screen. In *Rocky II* the hero falls down but eventually triumphs through rags-to-riches upward social mobility. Audiences cheer again. What will *Rocky III* have in store for us? More ups and downs, no doubt!

EARLY RESEARCH ON STRATIFICATION

Before examining the current stratification system in America, an overview of early social science research will be useful. Attention here is focused on what has been discovered about class and status stratification through classic studies, especially those of Robert and Helen Lynd, W. Lloyd Warner, and August Hollingshead.

The earliest American sociologists (Franklin Giddings, Albion Small, William Graham Summer, and Lester Ward) did not study stratification to any great extent. Charles Page (1969) and others have attributed this relative lack of concern to the fact that these sociologists were a product of their environment, an environment that did not tend to focus upon issues of inequality but instead emphasized the classlessness of American society.

Milton Gordon (1963) has pointed out that by the 1920s

there was a gradual increase in the study of stratification. This continued through the 1930s as the inequalities of wealth in America became very apparent during the Great Depression. A dominant influence during these two decades was the department of sociology at the University of Chicago. Under the leadership of such notables as Robert Park and Ernest Burgess, the city of Chicago became a veritable laboratory for sociological analysis. Important works by Nels Anderson, Franklin Frazier, Walter Reckless, Clifford Shaw, Louis Wirth, and Harvey Zorbaugh, among others, are included in this tradition. The primary mode of analysis in these studies was that of human ecology. The following statement by Park demonstrates the importance of stratification in this approach:

> One of the incidents of the growth of the community is the social selection and segregation of the population, and the creation, on the one hand, of natural social groups, and on the other of natural social areas (1926:8).

Park argued that groups differentiated on the basis of a number of social characteristics inhabit distinct residential areas. Among the characteristics which he mentioned that serve to separate groups residentially are what we have referred to as class stratification and status stratification. The connection between stratification position and residential location has been consistently demonstrated in research since the 1920s, and the so-called "ecological school" should be credited with focusing attention upon this important fact of stratification.

The Lynds

The studies entitled *Middletown* (1929) and *Middletown in Transition* (1937) by Robert and Helen Lynd also were carried out during the 1920s and 1930s. These far-reaching investigations examined the shape and character of a medium-sized midwestern city in Indiana.

Stratification entered into the Middletown research as a mode of analysis for interpreting patterns uncovered in different institutional structures such as the government, the educational system, the family, the churches, and the media. Although the pie of the stratification system was sliced in different ways in the Lynds' work, the prevailing picture of stratification was a twofold division entailing the basic split between a business class and a working class (Lynd and Lynd, 1929). Members of the business class, about 30 percent of the population, had jobs that centered around people. They sold and promoted anything ranging from cars (the salesmen) to ideas (the teachers). Working-class people, about 70 percent of the population, on the other hand, had jobs that revolved around things; and they used tools in their work.

An important question to ask is whether or not this profile of stratification represents class stratification or status stratification. Occupation, which was the Lynds' primary indicator of stratification position, can reflect either class stratification or status stratification. Throughout their work, the Lynds clearly were most interested in occupation as an index of class rather than of status position. Gordon (1963:69) has argued that the status aspects of stratification indeed were of secondary importance for the Lynds. Significant for their research was how the economic rewards of an individual's occupation had an impact upon the rest of one's life. The effect of such class stratification in Middletown was dramatic. "So the two worlds live; to each one the other is largely out of the picture" (Lynd and Lynd, 1929:478). The Lynds found that business-class people and working-class people not only lived in different neighborhoods; they also spent their leisure time differently, went to different churches, and sent their children to different schools.

The clear message of the Middletown studies is that a small number of families at the top of the business class called the shots and controlled the institutions of the city. They controlled the government by their influence over those who held public office. The role of campaign contributions entered in here. These key families in the business class also had a disproportionate impact upon the churches because church leaders depended upon their donations. The business class also influenced the educational institution greatly. For example, a leading member of the business class presided over the school board. Also, both of the newspapers in Middletown were dependent upon business-class money.

The net effect of such business-class influence was that viewpoints unfriendly to business-class interests were not often presented through the institutional structures of the community. As a result, the working class in Middletown did not develop any class consciousness. Even during the Depression, the American Dream Package (individualism, competition, the work ethic, social mobility, and success) was bought by the working class. This is startling, given the high unemployment and low income of the working class during this time.

Warner

If the major thrust of the Lynds' research was to examine class stratification, the corresponding accomplishment of Warner's research was to investigate status stratification through his classic studies of Yankee City (Warner and Lunt, 1941), a small city on the New England coast, and Jonesville (Warner and Associates, 1949), a small town in the Midwest.

What emerged from the research in Yankee City was a very influential profile of status stratification: a sixfold system comprised of upper, middle, and lower groupings, each of which had its own upper and lower segments (Warner, Meeker, and Eells, 1960:11-15). This system was based upon evaluations of where the residents of Yankee City fit into the total stratification system. These evaluations were made by a selected sample of Yankee City residents themselves. In other words, the reputational method of measuring stratification was employed.

At the top of the stratification system in Yankee City was the upper-upper status group—about one percent of the population—comprising the wealthy old families who had inherited their wealth. These families had been part of the upper-upper status group for several generations and knew and practiced the appropriate life style for upper-upper status people.

The lower-upper status families comprised roughly the same percentage of Yankee City's population. This group also possessed considerable wealth but did not have the family tradition of being a part of the upper-upper status group. The phrase "nouveaux riches" could be used to describe this group. Members of the group needed time to assimilate the life-style of the upper-upper status group and gradually be accepted. And it is interesting to note that the lower-upper status group actually had more wealth than the upper-upper status group. In other words, it was second in status but first in class. This indicates the discrepancy between class stratification and status stratification discussed earlier.

Another 10 percent of Yankee City was judged by town residents to be at the upper-middle status level. Successful businessmen and professionals were included in this group. Their incomes were less than those of the upper-status groups, but their orientation was towards eventual acceptance by the upper-status groups. One means for such acceptance was participation and leadership in community activities.

The upper-middle status group together with the two upper-status groups comprised what Warner referred to as "the Level above the Common Man." The Level of the Common Man included both the lower-middle status group and the upper-lower status group. Slightly over a quarter of Yankee City was in the lower-middle status group. Typical members were white-collar workers (excluding the successful professionals), the owners of some smaller businesses, and some of the skilled blue-collar workers. About a third of Yankee City was classified as falling into the other part of the Common Man level, the upper-lower status group. "Poor but honest workers," usually semiskilled or unskilled blue-collar workers, were ranked in this group.

Lastly, below the Level of the Common Man and at the bottom of the status hierarchy in Yankee City, was the 25 percent of the population classified as part of the lower-lower status group. These people often were unemployed and dependent upon relief or public welfare. When they did work, members of the lower-lower status group most often were employed in relatively unskilled blue collar positions. Comments on this group elicited from Yankee City residents generally were derogatory; accusations of sexual immorality and laziness were not uncommon.

The sixfold picture of status stratification in Yankee City also was found, with a minor exception, by Warner in Jonesville, the small Midwestern town. Here, the two upper-status groups were combined into a single status category, since a network of "wealthy old families" typical of older Eastern communities had not yet been formed. In any event, what becomes clear in the studies of both Yankee City and Jonesville is that status position had a decided impact upon the other aspects of one's life. As in the Middletown studies, the Jonesville study shows that position in the stratification system has a marked influence upon one's living conditions, one's associates, and what attitudes and behavior one expresses. Furthermore, members of the top stratification groups wield considerable power in the economic, political, and educational institutions of both Yankee City and Jonesville.

Hollingshead

Another classic study of stratification conducted during the 1940s is *Elmtown's Youth* (1949) by August Hollingshead. It revealed a five-layered status or prestige hierarchy in a midwestern community of approximately ten thousand persons. Hollingshead used the reputational approach in examining stratification, similar to the approach used by Warner. A capsule summary (Hollingshead, 1949:83-120) follows.

Group I *(less than one percent of the population)*
These families in Elmtown ranked highest in status. Family lineage and inheritance played prominent roles for them. Investments were an important source of their considerable wealth. They controlled large business and farming enterprises, but work was secondary to leisure.

Group II *(about five percent)*
These families were similar to the upper-middle group of Yankee City. Most successful professionals (doctors, lawyers, and dentists) were included in this group and aspired to gain membership in Group I by playing civic leadership roles. But they were well aware that the wealth of the first families was beyond their reach. What few investments they were able to make were made with an eye to economic security.

Group III *(about 25 percent)*
A substantial occupational spread was evident within this group: proprietors and some lower professionals, some farm owners, clerical and sales workers, and some craftsmen—in general, the more successful of the blue collar families. Viewed as being above

the level of the common man, they had little money for investment purposes but enough for the conveniences of life.

Group IV *(44 percent)*

Most blue collar workers and their families were classified here, the common man level of hard workers. They had enough money for basic necessities but very little for luxuries, and what money they did have typically was spent as soon as it was earned.

Group V *(about 25 percent)*

This was the lowest ranked group in Elmtown, below the level of the common man. Most were semi-skilled and unskilled workers or machine operators. Defined as immoral by the rest of the community, their incomes left many in the position of having to depend upon charity and public relief.

The above portrait of the stratification system is remarkably similar to the one drawn in Warner's research. However, *Elmtown's Youth* not only presents an important profile of stratification; it also serves as a benchmark study demonstrating the connection between stratification position and adolescent behavior. Most of the study focused upon how the stratification position of the youths affected them in the public-school system. Bias against children from lower stratification positions was quite evident. Informal social relations between students, such as dating relationships and friendships, were largely based upon family stratification background. Consequently, the net effect of the schools was to perpetuate the stratification system from one generation to the next.

The studies by the Chicago school, by the Lynds, by Warner and his associates, and by Hollingshead are considered classic works in American stratification research because they strongly influenced the course of research in the discipline. Other important studies by the earlier social scientists exist, of course; and any serious student of stratification would want to explore the works of Centers (1949) and Hunter (1953), among others. But the work of the Chicago school, the Lynds, Warner, and Hollingshead provide one with a firm grasp on what has been uncovered about stratification by earlier researchers. A question has to be raised, however: Are the findings of these earlier studies of stratification, done mostly in small towns thirty or more years ago, valid for urban America today?

THE CURRENT STRATIFICATION SYSTEM
IN THE UNITED STATES

As already mentioned, both Karl Marx and Max Weber, the two most important of the seminal minds in stratification analysis, saw economic factors as the prime determinants of social-class position. But each sketched more than one portrait of class, or economic, stratification. Weber argued that " 'Property' and 'lack of property' are, therefore, the basic categories of all class situations" (Weber, 1946:182). One can, however, according to Weber, make distinctions within these two groupings. Those with property can be distinguished according to the kind of property they have; those without property can be classified according to the kind of services that they perform in the economy.

Marx also gave more than one description of economic stratification. By far the best known depiction of class stratification in Marx's writing is his description in *The Communist Manifesto* (1948) of a basic split betwen capitalists (the bourgeoisie) and workers (the proletariat) in Western industrial societies. These two classes are differentiated on the basis of their relationship to the means of production—the property and equipment necessary for the production of goods and services in society. The capitalists own and control the means of production; the workers do not. Furthermore, workers must sell their labor power to others for a wage; capitalists do not, for they depend upon profits from their capital. Aside from this dichotomous model of class, Marx at times used a trichotomous model for analyzing class systems. For instance, he refers to a third major class of landowners in the last volume of *Capital* (1967:885). The two-class view of economic stratification, however, was paramount in his analysis.

The Class System

The task now is to apply the views of Marx and Weber regarding stratification to the current American class system. As was the case when Marx and Weber were writing, the class system today can be seen either from the standpoint of a twofold division or from the standpoint of multiple divisions. But in our view, the most appropriate description of the current class system in

America involves that of a basic split between an upper class and the non-upper class.

The upper class is made up of the top segment of the population in terms of economic benefits—primarily considerable wealth and high income. Previous research has estimated the size of the upper class in America as falling somewhere within the range of 0.2 percent to 3.0 percent of the population. This raises the questions of how and where one can draw the cutoff point for upper-class membership.

A fruitful approach to these questions is to look for a qualitative break in the distribution of something that is related to class position. The distribution of wealth in America provides such a discontinuity. In 1972 the net worth (the value of assets minus the value of liabilities) of the population was highly concentrated at the top. One percent of the population accounted for 25.9 percent of the total net worth of the population, *but* the top 0.5 percent had 20.4 percent of the net worth (U.S. Bureau of the Census, 1976:427). In a similar vein, 1.0 percent of the population owned 56.5 percent of the individually held corporate stock, *but* the top 0.5 percent owned 49.3 percent of the stock. These figures indicate a steep incline in the distribution of wealth in America that is accentuated towards those at the very top in the 0.5 percent position. Accordingly, we choose this 0.5 percent position in the distribution of wealth as the line of demarcation for upper-class membership. Therefore, 0.5 percent of the population is classified as upper class, while 99.5 percent is non-upper class.

How does income relate to upper-class membership? If we use annual income as a basic criterion for determining upper-class position, where should the cutoff point be? Should it be $200,000 or $100,000, $75,000 or $50,000? Once again, the top 0.5 percent position is chosen as the critical dividing point, but this time its is applied to the income distribution.

In 1975 0.5 percent of the American population had annual incomes of approximately $85,000 or more. A major reason for settling upon this point in the income distribution is that people at or above it derive a substantial part of their income from unearned sources, not salaries and wages, but sources such as stock and bond dividends. For example, those with incomes of $85,000 received, on the average, $30,000 from unearned sources.* Anderson and Gibson (1978:120) use $30,000 income from unearned sources as the line of demarcation for their capitalist class, which is similar to the upper class considered here. Again we are struck with the following two-class picture of the American population: 0.5 percent of the population is upper class, while 99.5 percent is non-upper class; that is, in 1975 they had annual incomes of less than $85,000.

Why are these economic groupings called social classes? As Anderson (1974:134) argues, ownership of corporate property gives an accurate measurement of class membership. The upper class owns approximately 50 percent of the individually held corporate stocks and bonds. The upper class is, therefore, the modern day equivalent of Marx's bourgeoisie class because its stock and bond ownership places it in the position of owning and controlling the means of production. Of course, there are signficant gradations within the upper classs. Heilbroner (1965: 26), for example, indicates that the top 150 corporations are, in the final analysis, under the control of between 200 and 300 families whose stock ownership gives them their power. This is practically the same as saying that a top, super-rich echelon of the upper class owns and controls the entire economy.

While it is frequently charged that the large corporations virtually control our lives, people often overlook that a very small group of upper-class people own and control these corporations. Such information is in direct conflict with publicly held beliefs which imply that the average American does own and can own even more of American industry. The Prudential Life Insurance Company conveys this notion through its TV commercial which contains the slogan, "Own a piece of the rock." We would footnote the commercial by noting that the piece of the rock will be small indeed. Clearly, the amount of corporate property in the hands of the non-upper class puts the non-upper class in a decidedly different position from that of the upper class.

---

*Both estimates are based on information presented in the I.R.S. publication entitled *Statistics of Income 1975, Individual Income Tax Returns,* Table 1.4, p. 13.

Another important way in which the upper class and the non-upper class can be contrasted is with respect to work. The jobs of upper-class people who do work clearly are much more desirable than those of non-upper class people in terms of income, status, and power; it is from upper class families that the rulers and the top managers of the key institutions in our society are recruited. One must remember, however, the basic reality that many upper class people do not have to work for a living. They do not have to sell their labor for survival. Once again, a very significant portion of their income, about 90 percent for families with an annual income of one million dollars or more, is derived from such unearned income as dividends from the stocks and bonds which they own.

Economically speaking, a job is of relatively minor importance to upper-class people. This means that the status and power associated with their jobs are primary reasons for their working, when they do work. Non-upper class people, on the other hand, depend upon their jobs for their income. They *do* have to sell their labor for survival. In contrast to the upper class, the overwhelming majority of the income for non-upper class people comes from wages, not unearned income. Non-upper class people clearly have to work for a living and can be viewed as the contemporary working class. This usage of the phrase "working class" is at variance with the more popular notion of the working class as the blue-collar world. We consider the non-upper class to be the working class both in the sense that its work is indispensable—its members must sell their labor and skill for survival—and in the Marxist sense that it does not own the means of production.

The upper class has been described with respect to its high levels of wealth and income, its ownership of corporate property, and its work situation. Similarly, the non-upper class has been characterized as having to work for survival, not owning decisive shares of corporate property, and having markedly less income and wealth than the upper class.

Why Only Two Classes? A major source of resistance to accepting this portrait of the American class structure is the belief that the class system is not polarized into two groups of haves and have-nots. To speak of a two-class model in contemporary America initially appears to fly in the face of conventional wisdom. It runs directly counter to the cherished belief in a broad, economically well-off "middle class" which acts as a buffer between the upper class and some lower class. A recent advocate of this credo is Wattenberg (1974) who argues that we have a "Massive Majority Middle Class." Of course, such declarations depend upon one's criteria. In the case of Wattenberg's analysis, the lower-income limit for a middle-class family in 1972 is $7,000. This hardly seems to be the financial formula for the "good life" in America today. More on this in Chapter 2.

It should be apparent from our review of the classic stratification studies of the Lynds, Warner, and Hollingshead that we are well aware of the prevalence of stratification models which contain more than two classes. One familiar with these and other studies might object to the two-class model because of the existence in America of "successful" and "well-off" white collar workers. Aside from doctors, lawyers and the like, this group includes the new technical, scientific, and professional workers—such as computer programmers and health technicians—sometimes referred to as the new working class. Are these people properly included in the non-upper class along with blue-collar workers and poor people?

A number of scholars sensitive to Marxist analysis speak to this question. Braverman (1974), for example, notes that there are middle strata between the upper class and the traditional working class. These strata take on some of the characteristics of both groups. Carchedi (1977) and Miliband (1977) attribute an "in-between" position to the new working class; it also takes on characteristics of both the upper class and the working class. Poulantzas (1975) gives a similar interpretation of the "new" petty bourgeoisie of clerical workers, supervisors, and salaried personnel in modern industry.

All of the above analysts describe the increasing proletarianization of middle-level workers in terms of their work role, but point out that there are differences between them and traditional blue-collar workers in areas such as salary and the degree of authority at work. All suggest, however, that these middle groups have more to gain by siding with the blue-collar working class than they do by lining up with the upper class. This supports the decision in this book to include the "in-between" groups as part of the non-upper class. It supports the view that, in fact, the "in between" groups have more in common with other non-upper class groups than they do with the upper class.

Some still will question the validity of this non-upper class by pointing out that the top part of it (for example, comfortable white-collar workers such as many doctors and lawyers) is in a situation devoid of economic exploitation. The response to this point is that the top part of the non-upper class is somewhat marginal. True enough, the top part of the non-upper class does have relatively high income, some corporate stock, and some unearned income. But the extent of these realities is different in kind from that in the upper class. The top part of the non-upper class does not own and control the means of production. The top part of the non-upper class must still work for survival even though its work situation may allow more freedom than do the jobs of others in the non-upper class such as typical factory work. It is also our contention that while there are important subdivisions within the non-upper class, for our purposes these subgroups can be combined with one another as the non-upper class because: 1) they are not upper class; and 2) they could benefit substantially from a redistribution of the wealth and power in America.

There is another reason why this book concentrates on the upper class and the extremely large non-upper class. It can be agreed that in any final showdown of the American class structure, some people from the top level of the non-upper class might side with the upper class. One of our purposes, however, is to consider the largest possible number of people who might confront the upper class. This, quite literally, is the 99.5 percent of the population which is not upper class—what this book calls the non-upper class. In other words, the two-class model is instructive from the standpoint of investigating a central theme of this book—upper class dominance—because if such dominance is to be challenged, a broad alliance of those who are not upper class must be formed. It is a step in the direction of consciousness raising to use the two-class model and from that perspective to see what hinders those who are not upper class from uniting and challenging the upper class.

As already indicated, there exists a variety of alternatives to the two-class system of class stratification just introduced. A standard one includes the following groups: an upper class, a middle class (with upper and lower segments), a working class (following the conventional blue-collar usage), and a lower class. Briefly, in this standard description of the class system, the upper class is roughly equivalent to what we have described as the upper class. The other "classes," however, are viewed as separate and distinct parts of what we have called the non-upper class. The middle class is usually described as the white-collar world and is considered to be relatively well-off financially. The working class is defined as the blue-collar world, less secure economically; and the lower class is equated with a poverty category in America. These different groups virtually parallel those sketched by Warner in his studies of Yankee City and Jonesville. This book maintains Warner's assertion that these non-upper class groups fundamentally reflect differences in status or prestige, rather than class or economic condition. Accordingly, it will consider further this "standard" picture of American class stratification under the rubric of the status system.

The Status System

As stated earlier, status is the level of prestige granted to families or individuals on the basis of who or what they are. Weber (1946:180-195) elaborates upon this conception of status by suggesting that in any society there exists a hierarchy of status groups, each made up of people with a similar level of prestige. Each status group tends to interact with only its own status group members. Accordingly, neighborhoods, friendship groups, and mate selection for marriage reflect this tendency to stay with one's own kind and exclude outsiders. Also, each status group exhibits a distinctive life-style. Each status group possesses its own set of attitudes, practices, and definition of what is "in." In regard to this, Weber places special emphasis upon the role of consumption as a mechanism by which each status group symbolizes its position. Hence, the phrase "status symbol." Finally, any status system can be thought of as a pecking order, with those higher in the hierarchy likely to have feelings of superiority and those near the bottom more likely to have feelings of inferiority.

Four groups comprise the current status system: the elite, the white-collar world, the blue-collar world, and the poor. For all intents and purposes, the same 0.5 percent of the population that makes up what we have called the upper class is also the elite. The term *elite* denotes the top of the status system. Discussing the elite is, in essence, discussing the status factor in the lives of upper-class people.

Inherited wealth, a family name such as Rockefeller or Dupont, and tradition hallmark the elite in America today. This is not to say the people who have accumulated a vast amount of money in their own lifetimes cannot ascend into the elite. Some do; but, when they do, they rarely define what the elite's life-style will be. Rather, they can share in the existing life-style of the elite.

The life-style of the elite has been well documented by Baltzell (1958) and Domhoff (1970). Briefly stated, the elite enjoys what most would consider the "best" life-style in America today. They have the material means to consume the best and the most—mansions, luxury cars, expensive and extensive travel. They have the leisure to "dabble in the arts." They have the most freedom in economic, social, and psychological terms.

In addition to the above, the elite has a life-style that entails exclusive interaction with members of the elite. The residential areas they choose are either in exclusive suburban areas or in the most desirable sections of major central cities—Park Avenue in New York, for example. Placement of the children of the elite in prep schools such as Groton, St. Paul's, and Hotchkiss, among a few others, ensures the perpetuation of the elite's privileged position into the next generation. Graduation from such schools virtually guarantees acceptance at one of the prestigious Ivy League colleges and membership in the appropriate elite clubs at such institutions. Huntington Hartford of the A. & P. fortune has commented that although he was just a C-student at St. Paul's, he was automatically accepted at Harvard. It is difficult to imagine a C-student at a typical high school being able to do the same thing.

A system of clubs in the key cities of America has an elite membership. Good examples are the New Orleans Club in Boston, the Links in New York, and the Pacific Union in San Francisco. These are all private men's clubs. A parallel set of clubs also exists for women of the elite. Final elements in the pattern of exclusive, elite interaction are the very posh and private resort areas where only the elite congregate and recreate. The system of residential areas, schools, clubs, and vacation spots insures an overall situation where elite people have contact only with other elite people. Consequently, this maintains a distance between the elite and those beneath the elite in the status hierarchy.

Below the elite are the other three major status groups in America: the white-collar world, the blue-collar world, and the poor. Pointed out above was that these groups often are thought of as classes rather than status groups. Although there arise some significant economic differences between these groups (to be discussed in Chapter 2), their different levels of prestige serve as the basic differential. This differential appears most strongly on the dimension of occupational prestige.

The major division in the prestige hierarchy of occupations comes between white-collar work and blue-collar work. Briefly, white-collar work emphasizes mind over body, mental activity over physical activity, brains over brawn. Blue-collar work, on the other hand, stresses the body—physical activity, and brawn. Significant gradations emerge within each of these two categories of work. The white-collar world ranges from successful professionals at the top to clerical help at the bottom. In the blue-collar world, the hierarchy encompasses both the highly-skilled craftsmen at the top and the unskilled laborers at the bottom. Nevertheless, one of the most consistent sociological research findings is that white-collar workers are granted considerably more prestige than blue-collar workers in American society. In both 1947 (North and Hatt) and 1963 (Hodge, Siegel, and Rossi) results from the National Opinion Research Center surveys showed this to be the case. A representative sample of the US population consistently ranked white-collar occupations such as scientist, lawyer, dentist, civil engineer, and accountant far above blue-collar occupations such as plumber, coal miner, janitor, bartender, and barber. Interestingly, the majority of Americans do not participate in the white-collar world. In fact, as Levison (1974) and others have pointed out, a careful examination of the US occupational structure reveals that the blue-collar world employs considerably more people than the white-collar world.

Who are the poor? The poor live at the subsistence level or below in terms of food, clothing, shelter, and medical care— in short, the basic necessities of life. The poor can be operationally defined as that group of individuals whose incomes fall at or below the poverty line established by the federal government ($5,500 for a family of four in 1975). This means that the poor make up the bottom part of the non-upper class. Such economic realities are readily translated into status stigmata as well. That they do not have adequate clothing, shelter, and medical care facilitates a consensus that the poor are unworthy. To be categorized as unworthy sums up what it means to be at the bottom of the status hierarchy in America. It means to be looked down upon, treated as inferior, and blamed for one's situation.

An important fact, lost sight of by many, is that most of the poor do work, but at jobs within the sphere of the blue-collar world—usually semiskilled or unskilled position. This raises a problem in any attempt to summarize the status system. Should the poor who work at blue-collar positions be classified as part of the blue-collar world? Our decision is to treat the poor as a separate status group because of their low position in the status hierarchy. Included as part of the blue-collar world are only those people who both work at blue-collar jobs and are above the poverty level. With these provisos in mind, the current status structure in America breaks down roughly in the following way:

.5%	elite
35.0%	white collar
50.0%	blue collar
14.5%	poor

Further discussion of status realities for the white-collar world, the blue-collar world, and the poor (the nonelite groups) can be found in Chapters 3, 4, and 5.

The Relationship Between the Class and Status Systems

The difference between class stratification and status stratification has been mentioned earlier. This dichotomy can imply a number of things. A person does not necessarily occupy the same economic and status positions. Examples of this included the member of organized crime and the teacher. One might also point out the case in which some white-collar workers have more prestige but less income than some highly skilled blue-collar workers. The frequency of such inconsistencies declines, however, when dealing with a two-level class system and a status system with four groups.

DIAGRAM 1

Class System	Status System
upper class	elite
non-upper class	nonelite: white collar blue collar poor

As the above diagram shows, there is consistency at the top and at the bottom of the stratification system. Most, if not all, upper-class families are part of the elite, while most, if not all, non-upper class families are part of the nonelite.

Class stratification and status stratification are related in another way: if one dominates the beliefs about stratification in a particular society, the other is likely to be obscured. This appears to be the case in American society which places great stress upon status stratification. The upper-class-influenced media encourages Americans to be a nation of "status seekers." Americans want to "move up" in status, as the advertisements and commercials imply they will if they buy this car or that liquor. In a similar way, much time is spent trying to "keep up with the Joneses" and scrambling to "get ahead" by a variety of ploys relying on one-upmanship in the areas of educational attainment, occupational advancement, and leisure time pursuits. The persistent desire to improve our level of status motivates these struggles. Consequently, Americans appear to be primarily status conscious rather than class conscious. They notice invidious status distinctions (what the latest "in" or "trendy" consumer item is) rather than the gross class differences that exist between the upper class and the non-upper class. In sum, Americans emphasize status differences, and this contributes in a major way to insuring that consciousness of the two-class system is relatively undeveloped.

THE PERSISTENCE OF AMERICAN STRATIFICATION

A comparison of the findings from earlier research with the current stratification system in America reveals continuities. Even though earlier studies of stratification were done mostly in small towns or cities thirty or more years ago, their results parallel current knowledge about stratification in America. Current research, for example, continues to demonstrate the decided impact that stratification position has upon practically every phase of one's existence, ranging from where one lives to how one spends his or her leisure time. Furthermore, the proportions of the status system remain virtually identical. The percentage of today's population that is part of the blue-collar world, for example, is almost the same as that when Warner carried out his studies. The same can be said about the elite and white-collar segments of the status hierarchy. Finally, the impact of those at the top of the stratification system has remained the same. As in earlier reserch, there still exists a small upper class that controls the economic institution and that, through its economic power, asserts its influence on other key institutions such as the government, education, and the media. *Plus ca change, plus c'est la meme chose* [the more things change, the more they are the same].

If, in fact, there has not been significant change in the stratification system of the US over time, the following questions must be asked again: Why does social inequality persist in

America? What allows such large economic differences to exist in our society? What prevents non-upper class America from demanding and achieving change in the distribution of income, wealth, and power? In an effort to answer these questions, the remaining chapters of the book are organized around the major obstacles that non-upper class America faces in accomplishing change.

Chapter 2 centers around an in-depth discussion of the extent to which income, wealth, and power are concentrated in America and how this concentration tends to perpetuate itself, thereby reducing this possibility of egalitarian change. In Chapter 3, Americans' understandings of stratification and the realities of the stratification system are compared and contrasted. Chapter 4 directs attention to the splits and divisions, both within and between non-upper class groups, which tend to keep the non-upper class divided. In Chapter 5, the key institutions in America are explored from the stand-point of how they obscure the reality of stratification and perpetuate the existing stratification system. Finally, Chapter 6 considers a variety of political options for dealing with the concentration of income, wealth, and power.

THE CONCENTRATION OF WEALTH, INCOME, AND POWER

The very rich are different from you and me.
Yes, they have more money.
　　　　Ernest Hemingway

The significance of this response in the story "The Snows of Kilimanjaro" to the comment that the rich, or upper class, are different is usually lost. Overlooked is the extent, depth, and breadth of their economic advantage over the rest of the population. With this in mind, let us look at the income level of the upper class.

Income is defined as the amount of money that an individual or family receives during a given year. The sources of income can be either earned or unearned. Earned income derives primarily from salaries and wages; an example of unearned income is dividends from stockownership. The income distribution in America shows a substanstial concentration at the top. In 1975, for example, the highest 20 percent of all families took home a little over 40 percent of the total income received by all families in that year (US Bureau of the Census, 1976: 406). During the same year, the top 5 percent of families received slightly more than 15 percent of the total income taken in by all families. These income statistics include some non-upper class members as well as the upper class.

THE INCOME OF THE UPPER CLASS

Of prime concern is the concentration of income in the upper class as previously defined. Anyone with an annual income of

$85,000 is considered part of the upper class. This means that approximately 0.5 percent of the American population is upper class. Rossides (1976:131) presents income data that come closer to dealing with the upper class than the data cited above. In 1971 the highest one percent of families accounted for 7.5 percent of all family income received in America. Now, if perfect equality existed, each one percent of the population would take home one percent of the total income. Therefore, the top one percent of the American population receives approximately seven and a half times as much income as it would if perfect equality existed. If we limit our focus to the upper class alone—the top 0.5 percent of the population—the income concentration is even greater. Judging from a variety of government data, it is safe to estimate that the upper-class share of the national income is at least ten times its proportion of the population.

Having looked at these data in the aggregate, we will now examine who some upper-class individuals are. High on the list, but not at the very top, are the chief executives of the leading corporations in America. For example, in 1976 Rawleigh Warner Jr., the chief executive of Mobil Oil, received a total remuneration of $717,000 and John Riccardo of Chrysler received $700,000 (*Forbes*, 1977:244). These incomes are clearly astronomical in comparison with the $15,001 that the average American family earned in the same year. In fact, the yearly incomes of the leading corporations' chief executives are much larger than the lifetime earnings of the average American family. Given this, it is difficult to comprehend that most of the chief executives are not at the very top of the income distribution. Their yearly remunerations do not put them securely in the $1,000,000 and above income category.

Who is at this level? What seems startling is that there are people such as J. Paul Getty, who made $300,000 *each day*, on the pinnacle of the income pyramid. The extent of economic stratification in America today can be summed up by the following comparison: the income of the average American family is surpassed by the income of the chief executive of General Motors ($966,000 in 1976) in the same way that the latter's income is outdistanced by the income of those at the very top of the income hierarchy. In other words, not only is there a big difference between upper-class incomes and non-upper class incomes, there is also substantial variation in income within the upper class.

Very important for understanding the highest echelon of the income distribution—the $1,000,000 and above category—is to note that what predominates at this level is unearned income rather than earned income. In 1975, slightly less than 90 percent of the income reported on US tax returns for this income grouping came from unearned sources such as the dividends from stock and bond ownership (Internal Revenue Service, 1978:13). A legitimate question to ask is whether or not upper-class people at this level of income worked for their ownership of such unearned sources of income. The answer given by Lundberg (1968:132) is clear. Practically all large incomes in America are based upon the inheritance of unearned income sources which allows for the perpetuation of high income from generation to generation of upper-class families.

The discussion of upper-class income so far has emphasized the higher echelons of the upper class. What about other upper class individuals who are not at the very top of the income pyramid? As indicated earlier, the lowest point in the income distribution that included upper-class people in 1975 was $85,000. The average individual with this amount of income clearly was not in the same position as the Duponts. But, as indicated in Chapter 1, such persons did receive $30,000 from unearned income sources. This placed them in a very comfortable position, compared with non-upper class Americans, because it meant that their incomes were substantially rooted in non-work sources such as dividends, interest payments, business ownership, and the like.

The discussion of the part that unearned income sources play in the economic lives of upper-class Americans naturally leads to an examination of the wealth accumulated by them. As will be seen shortly, the wealth concentration in the upper class is even more dramatic than the income concentration.

THE WEALTH OF THE UPPER CLASS

The **wealth** of an individual or family is the economic worth of everything that it owns: stocks, real estate, cash, bonds, cars, trusts, insurance, etc. The term used to indicate the total value of all such assets minus the value of liablities is **net worth,** a good index of overall wealth. It is difficult to obtain recent and precise information on the net worth of the upper class. According to James Smith (1974:143-180), as of 1969 only 0.1 percent of adult Americans had a net worth of $1,000,000 or more. In other words, very few people have realized the American Dream of being a millionaire. Nevertheless, the upper class is not far from the millionaire level. Thurow and Lucas (1972:12) show that in 1962 the top 0.5 percent of American families had a net worth of $500,000 or more. It is safe to assume that upper-class wealth has not declined in absolute terms since then.

How does the upper class share of the nation's total wealth compare with its share of the total income? The data presented in Table 1 allow an assessment. About a fifth of the total net worth of the entire population is accounted for by the upper class, the top 0.5 percent. This wealth concentration gives the upper class a slice of the pie which is roughly twice as large as its already very large income share. In short, the income concentration pales by comparison with the wealth concentration. The upper-class advantage over the rest of the population is even greater with respect to wealth than it is with regard to income.

Although the upper class has a fifth of the total population's net worth, it owns a far greater share of the total population's assets in some specific categories. For example, the data in Table 1 show that in 1972 the top 0.5 percent of the population, the upper class, accounted for approximately 80 percent of all trusts. This fact reflects the attempt on the part of the upper class to minimize the effect of taxation on its wealth, so that upper-class members can pass on their economic advantage to their sons, daughters, and other relatives.

At the very heart of class (economic) stratification is the ownership, or non-ownership , and control, or non-control, of the means of production—the property and equipment necessary for the production of goods and services in society. As mentioned in Chapter 1, a very good index of the ownership

TABLE 1
Concentration of Wealth in 1972

| | *Percent owned by* | |
Asset	Top ½ percent	Top 1 percent
Net worth	20.4	25.9
Trusts	80.8	89.0
Bonds	52.2	60.0
Corporate stock	49.3	56.5
Debt instruments	39.1	52.7
Real estate	10.1	15.1
Cash	8.5	13.5
Life insurance	4.3	7.0

Source: U.S. Bureau of the Census, *Statistical Abstract of the United States.* 1976, Table 694, p. 427.

and control of the means of production is the ownership of individually-held corporate stocks and bonds. As already seen, the upper class owns approximately half of the bonds and corporate stock. For all intents and purposes, this reflects upper-class ownership and control of corporate America.

Finally, the data above highlight the point that there is a big difference in wealth between the top 0.5 percent, the upper class, and those immediately below them. For example, while the top one percent of the population owns 89.9 percent of the trusts, the top 0.5 percent alone controls 80.8 percent. A similar dominance by the top 0.5 percent of the other assets listed is also apparent. The top 0.5 percent makes the second 0.5 percent look poor by comparison. This hints at the extent of economic stratification between upper-class and non-upper class America, the major stratification cleavage in the United States. With this in mind, attention now shifts to non-upper class America.

A PROFILE OF NON-UPPER CLASS AMERICA

Non-upper class America has been described previously as consisting of three major status groupings: the white-collar world (35 percent), the blue-collar world (50 percent), and the poor (14 percent). This profile of the non-upper class challenges one of the most widely held beliefs about America, namely that the majority of the population is employed in white-collar occupations. Consequently, some explanation of the percentages classified as white collar, blue collar, and poor is necessary.

The data presented below by the US Bureau of Labor Statistics show that a little over 40 percent of the male* labor force in 1975 was classified as white collar. A slightly larger percentage, roughly 45 percent, was classified as blue collar. However,

TABLE 2

Occupations of Male Labor Force in 1975

Occupational Group	
Total	51,230,000
White Collar	21,134,000
Professional and Technical	7,481,000
Managers and Administrators	7,162,000
Salesworkers	3,137,000
Clerical workers	3,355,000
Blue Collar	23,220,000
Craft and kindred workers	10,472,000
Operatives	8,971,000
Nonfarm laborers	3,777,000
Service workers	4,400,000
Farmworkers	2,476,000

Source: U.S. Bureau of the Census, *Statistical Abstract of the United States:* 1976, Table 600, p. 372.

---

*It is legitimate to ask why only data for the male population are being considered. The main reason for this is that even though an increasing number of women are working today, the evidence still suggests that the occupation of the male head of household serves to define the status identification for most American families. Levison (1974), for example, illustrates that families where the husband is a blue-collar worker and the wife is a white-collar worker have an identification that is more blue collar than white collar. In brief, the male occupational structure gives a quite accurate picture of non-upper class America.

it is necessary to make adjustments of these data because they contain a tendency to overestimate how many white-collar workers there are and underestimate the number of blue-collar workers. One such modification concerns the white-collar classification. While it can be agreed that the occupational groupings of professional and technical, managers and administrators, salesworkers, and clerical workers are most appropriately categorized as white collar, in which the mind is emphasized more than the body, there are important exceptions. As Levison (1974:23) points out, the clerical and sales categories hide within them the specific jobs of newsboys, office machine operators, and baggagemen, among others, which are more properly considered as part of the blue-collar world. In a similar way, some jobs that are classified in the professional groupings are better thought of as blue collar. A case in point is the job of acrobat which is included under the professional category by the *Dictionary of Occupational Titles.* The emphasis upon the body in the work of an acrobat makes it dubious to us that acrobats are white collar rather than blue collar. If such jobs are eliminated from the white-collar category, a more accurate estimate of the percentage of white-collar workers in America is possible. A good estimate would be in the range of 30 to 35 percent of the male labor force. To be on the safe side, we will use the 35 percent figure.

Very important adjustments in the above data need to be made regarding the blue-collar grouping. First, the jobs mistakenly considered as white collar above have to be reclassified as blue collar. Furthermore, the category of service workers should be treated as blue collar. The overwhelming majority of specific jobs in this category (for example, cooks, busboys, firemen, and guards) are manual by nature. They stress physical activity over mental activity. The same rationale can be made for the category of farmworkers. By classifying farmworkers and service workers as blue collar, the total number classified as blue collar jumps considerably.

Before making an estimate of the actual percentage of the male labor force properly considered as blue collar, some comments must be interjected about the status group of the poor. As of 1975, about 12 percent of the US population was at or below the poverty level established by the federal government.

This is a very conservative estimate of the extent of poverty in America: Others range between 15 and 20 percent. Our compromise estimate is 14.5 percent. This has a bearing on the blue-collar estimate because we have decided to include as part of the blue-collar world only those who both work at blue-collar jobs and are above the poverty level. Most of the poor do work at blue-collar jobs, usually in the semiskilled or unskilled positions. However, because of their uniquely low position in the status hierarchy, the poor are not included in the overall blue-collar category. For these reasons, the blue-collar estimate is 50 percent, instead of 64.5 percent of the population.

THE INCOME OF THE NON-UPPER CLASS

Now that a profile of the different segments, or status groups, within non-upper class America has been sketched, an analysis of the economic realities of the non-upper class is appropriate.

Anyone with an annual income of less than $85,000 in 1975* is included in the non-upper class. This means that there is much variation in the incomes of non-upper class people. But, the variation is not as great as first might be suspected because there is a marked tendency for the majority of the non-upper class to have incomes considerably less than $85,000. This tendency can clearly be seen when one examines the average income of American families. The median income, a good estimate of average income, was $13,772 for American families in 1975. Recall that if we eliminated the incomes of upper class people, the median income of just non-upper class people would be reduced somewhat.

What about the income levels of the different status groups

---

*The data on income and wealth are unavoidably dated to some extent. The effort has been made to obtain data for 1975 so that they will be as recent and comparable as possible. The temptation might exist to disregard what the information suggests, namely that most Americans are economically squeezed. One might ask, "What about today? Things may have been bad then, but what about now?" The answer is that things have gotten worse economically for most Americans since 1975. One reason for this is that inflation has outpaced rises in the incomes of workers between 1975 and now.

TABLE 3
Median Earnings of Male* Workers in 1975

Occupational Group

White Collar

Professional and Technical	$ 15,796
Managers and Administrators	$ 15,787
Salesworkers	$ 13,840
Clerical workers	$ 12,096

Blue Collar

Craft and kindred workers	$ 12,588
Operatives	$ 11,006
Service workers	$ 9,488
Nonfarm laborers	$ 9,057

Source: U.S. Bureau of the Census, *Statistical Abstract of the United States:* 1977, Table 663, p. 411.

within the non-upper class (the white-collar world, the blue-collar world, and the poor)? The poor are readily defined as the group at the bottom of the income distribution. The federal government establishes a point in the income distribution as the cutoff level for who is considered poor or non-poor. In 1975, this was approximately $5,000 for a family of four people.

The income ranges for the white-collar and blue-collar groups are more difficult to identify. Nevertheless, a number of points can be made. First, white-collar incomes are generally higher than blue-collar incomes. Examination of the data above confirm this point. On the other hand, it is also apparent that some blue-collar workers make higher incomes than some white-collar workers. In 1975, for example, male craft and kindred workers had a higher median income than did male clerical workers. In other words, the top of the blue-collar world had higher incomes than the bottom of the white-collar world.

---

*The major difference between the data for males and females is that the income levels for women are lower than those for men in each occupational category.

The overlap of the white-collar and blue-collar worlds does not remove, however, the overall inequity between their incomes. The professional, technical, and managerial workers at the top of the white-collar world still have significantly higher incomes than the top of the blue-collar world. It should also be kept in mind that fringe benefits are generally better for white-collar workers than for blue-collar workers.

While there are income differences within the non-upper class between the white-collar world, the blue-collar world, and the poor, they all share an important thing in common. Their incomes are in a different league from the incomes of upper-class Americans. There are no Rockefellers in their midst.

Let's attempt to draw out the significance of the income levels of non-upper class America. In particular, what does the median income figure of $13,772 in 1975 mean to the average American family whether it be white collar or blue collar? A question has to be asked: Is $13,772 enough to live on comfortably? One gauge for answering this question is provided by the Bureau of Labor Statistics. Every year the Bureau makes estimates of how much it costs to live at three different levels of living: a lower budget, an intermediate budget, and a higher budget.

A look at the intermediate budget reveals that it is quite modest indeed (Levison, 1974:32-33). It assumes that a family living on such a budget will buy a two-year-old *used* car and keep it for four years. The toaster in the kitchen must last for 33 years. The budget includes no money for savings. The intermediate budget is decidedly not for a high life-style and yet most non-upper class people cannot afford it. In 1975 the estimate for the intermediate budget for a family of four was $15,318 in urban areas, $15,638 in metropolitan areas, and $13,886 in nonmetropolitan areas (US Bureau of the Census, 1976:443). Once again, the median income for American families in 1975 was $13,772 overall, and somewhat lower in non-metropolitan areas. This strongly suggests that there is a significant difference between the income non-upper class people receive and what they actually need.

The gap between what non-upper class people can afford and what they need is nowhere more clearly illustrated than in the area of housing. According to the M.I.T.-Harvard Joint Center for Urban Studies, the percentage of American families able to afford a medium priced new house in 1977 was 27 percent. Things have not improved since 1977. At one point in 1980, only 5 percent of the American population could afford to buy an average-priced house.

A much closer estimate of what it actually cost for a comfortable level of family living in 1975 is $35,000. By comfortable level of living, we do not mean an extravagant level by any means. Rather, comfortable here is equated with the conventional "middle class" life-style—a decent house, a workable car, provisions for the education of children, etc. Clearly, the average non-upper class family in America with an income of $13,772 was not able to support such a life-style. A more accurate picture of life for such people is that they must struggle from paycheck to paycheck—not in the same sense as the poor struggle; but, nevertheless, struggle is the appropriate word. One gets the image of most families in the non-upper class working very hard, many with two wage earners, and still not coming close to achieving the comfortable level of existence that is held before them like a carrot by the media. Television commercials, for example, constantly suggest that most Americans have achieved the conventional "middle class" life-style.

If the average non-upper class family has to struggle from paycheck to paycheck, what must life be like for the poor who had to live on $5,500 a year or less? The situation for poor Americans is almost incomprehensible. The fact that a great deal of dog food is eaten by poor people underlines the extent of their plight. Their situation with respect to housing, clothing, education, and medical care is similar to their situation with respect to food. The poor truly must struggle to survive on a *day to day* basis.

As mentioned in Chapter 1, the facts of economic stratification in America are hard to reconcile with Wattenberg's (1974) portrait of an affluent middle-class society. That he sets the lower income limit for a middle-class family in 1972 at $7,000 deserves no further comment. It should be clear by now that the word *affluent* is one to be reserved for descriptions of the upper class and not for characterizations of the non-upper class.

THE WEALTH OF THE NON-UPPER CLASS

So far the income situation of the non-upper class has been discussed. A striking contrast between its situation and that of the upper class can be seen. A similar contrast can be drawn regarding wealth. As mentioned previously, upper-class people have a net worth of $500,000 or more. The wealth distribution of the non-upper class is presented in Table 4.

TABLE 4

Wealth of Non-Upper Class Population in 1969

Net Worth	*Percent of Adult Non-Upper Class Population*
$ 100,000 – $ 500,000	2.4
$ 60,000 – $ 100,000	1.7
$ 40,000 – $ 60,000	3.1
$ 20,000 – $ 40,000	6.5
$ 10,000 – $ 20,000	10.0
$ 5,000 – $ 10,000	13.0
$ 3,000 – $ 5,000	13.0
Less than $ 3,000	50.2

Source: James Smith, Steven Franklin, and Douglas Wion, "Distribution of Financial Assets," in *In the Pockets of a Few,* ed. Fred Harris. New York: Grossman, 1974.

A number of points should be stressed about these data. First of all, there are some fairly well-off people at the top of the non-upper class. About 4 percent of the population has a net worth ranging from $60,000 to $500,000. These people, however, are clearly in a different league from the upper class with regard to wealth. Approximately 10 percent of the non-upper class has a net worth between $20,000 and $60,000. Their wealth might be described as modest. For the 23 percent of the population whose net worth is between $5,000 and $20,000, the word *meager* is most appropriately used in characterizations of their wealth. What is staggering is that 63 percent of the American population has a net worth of less than $5,000. In truth, it is a question as to whether or not they own the clothes on their backs. They live in near destitution.

Note that the data on wealth presented above do not compare the different status groups within the non-upper class (the white-collar world, the blue-collar world, and the poor). Data for this purpose are not available. Nevertheless, it is safe to say that the poor come out on the bottom of the wealth hierarchy. Some few top white-collar and blue-collar people may have impressive net worths, but they are not in the driver's seat of the economy by any means. Indeed, the above data strongly suggest that most white-collar and blue-collar people have very humble situations when it comes to wealth.

One can make interesting comparisons regarding the types of assets that upper class and non-upper class people own. First, from data presented earlier (see page 29), it is already known that the upper class owns about one half of the individually held stocks and bonds. The non-upper class owns the other half of the stocks and bonds; but the dispersal of its half among 99.5 percent of the population renders its "ownership" ineffective and, for all intents and purposes, nonexistent. Accordingly, we state again that the upper class owns the means of production and the non-upper class does not.

Projector and Weiss (1962:110) bring out another wealth comparison of the upper class and the non-upper class. In 1962 the upper class, with $500,000 or more in net worth, had about one half of its net worth tied up in investments, but only 4.5 percent in homes and 0.2 percent in cars. The bottom wealth group ($1-$999 in net worth), on the other hand, had 48 percent of its money involved in automobile ownership while those with a net worth of $5,000-$24,999 had over 50 percent of their wealth connected to home ownership. In order to draw out the meaning of these statistics fully, one must remember that the upper-class person drives the Rolls-Royce while the non-upper class person drives a Chevrolet. Furthermore, the homes of the upper class are palatial in comparison with the dwellings of the non-upper class. These contrasts are true even though the upper class does not spend that much of its money on cars and homes, whereas the non-upper class does.

How can we sum up the picture of the non-upper class when it comes to income and wealth? Far from enjoying a comfortable and easy existence, most people in America struggle for economic survival to one degree or another. Furthermore, the non-upper class does not own the means of production. As a consequence, virtually all non-upper class people must work at jobs where alienation and deadly accidents are not uncommon just in order to attempt economic survival.

TAXATION AND CLASS POSITION

The non-upper class also suffers from the burden of taxation, which for them is tyranny. Taxation must be taken into account because the ultimate economic reward that one receives is what remains after taxes. The system of taxation in America accomplishes this determination of economic reward in a manner that is highly favorable to the upper class and highly unfair to the non-upper class.

One of the accepted guidelines for taxation in America is **progressivity**. This means that those who are well-off should pay taxes at a higher rate than those who are not as well-off. In reality most taxes in America are **regressive**—they hit segments of the non-upper class harder than they affect the upper class. Stern (1972) and others have indicated that state income taxes, local property taxes, the federal social security tax, and sales taxes all tend to be regressive. A classic illustration is the social security tax. In 1975 all workers had to pay 5.85 percent of their first $14,100 in income for social security. Nothing was taxed for social security on income above $14,100. Consequently, a worker with an income of $14,100 had to pay 5.85 percent of it for social security. But, someone with an income of $100,000 also had to pay 5.85 percent of the first $14,100 of income for social security. And, someone with an income of $1,000,000 also had to pay the same amount as the person who made $14,100. As a result, the upper class bypassed the progressivity principle.

The federal income tax deserves special attention. On paper, but not in practice, the federal income tax is quite progressive. In 1974 families with incomes near the median income ($13,772) theoretically had to pay a federal income tax amounting to approximately 20 percent of their income. Families with incomes of $200,000 or more theoretically had to pay a federal income tax of 55 percent of their first $200,000 and 70 percent of their income beyond $200,000. The federal income tax system, however, also includes a number of loopholes which enable primarily upper-class people to pay nowhere near the amount that they would otherwise have to pay. Stern (1972:11) provides a clear illustration of these tax loopholes. A family with an annual income of under $3,000 is saved $16 by the tax loopholes. The family with a yearly income in the range of $10,000-$15,000 receives $651 savings as a result of the loopholes. But, the average family with an income of over $1,000,000 saves an incredible $720,490.

The degree to which inequality exists in the federal income-tax system deserves further documentation. In 1974, there were 244 individuals with incomes over $200,000 who paid no taxes. They would have paid taxes at a rate of somewhere between 55 percent and 70 percent if the loopholes did not exist. A prime example of the seeming underpayment of taxes by upper class people was the case of J. Paul Getty who, with a *daily* income of $300,000, used to pay a few thousand dollars in *yearly* taxes. Without the loopholes, Getty would have paid seventy million dollars a year in taxes. Another example, of course, is Richard Nixon who, as the president of the United States, claimed illegal deductions and paid the same federal income tax as someone with a $7,000 annual income. As president, Nixon earned $200,000. Clearly, the upper class benefits to an unbelievable extent from the federal income tax system.

Consider also that for years the Internal Revenue Service has directed its attention to pursuing the tax illegalities of non-upper class families with incomes near the median income figure and not upper-class families who have been shown to be responsible for far greater tax illegalities. Indeed, many non-upper class people might be caught saying the taxpayer's prayer of Russell Baker near every April fifteenth.

O mighty Internal Revenue, who turneth the labor of man to ashes, we thank thee for the multitude of thy forms which thou hast

set before us and for the infinite confusion of thy commandments
which multiplieth the fortunes of lawyer and accountant alike . . . .

Let Monday and Tuesday of every week satisfy thee, O great
taxers. Grant that we not be asked to give thee Wednesday, too.
Look upon our oil bills and take not our Wednesdays, we pray thee.

If we offend thee, stay thy fury. Send not thy dread agents with
their powerful liens to seize our cars and our places of abode and our
pants . . . .

Look upon us, O Internal Revenue, and see our terror, and know
that thou art mighty while we are mere impecunious clay on a dark
passage from earned income to Social Security with no tax shelter
to protect us along the way (1977:12).

Of late there has been considerable reaction on the part of
non-upper class people against the sytem of taxation in
America. These reactions have come from a variety of positions
on the political spectrum. The success of both President Carter's
1976 campaign description of the tax system as "a disgrace to
the human race" and California's Proposition 13 in 1978 are
two such examples. Proposals that seek to alter the US system
of taxation will be commented on further in Chapter 6.

THE AMERICAN ECONOMY AND THE UPPER CLASS

It has already been argued that the upper class in America
owns and controls the means of production through its stock
ownership. The purpose here is to clarify the nature of the
economic system controlled and the process of its control
by the upper class.

Just as a large percentage of wealth and income is concentrated in the hands of a small percentage of the population—the
upper class—a similarly high degree of concentration can be
discerned in American corporations. For example, if we
examine the top 500 corporations, it becomes apparent that
the profits of the top ten are almost equivalent with the profits
of the next 490 (Heilbroner, 1965:10). Also, in 1969 the 200
largest corporations accounted for 60 percent of all manufacturing assets, while the top one hundred firms had 48 percent of
such assets (Anderson, 1974:211-212). These statistics suggest

the pyramid structure of American corporations. Essentially, a relatively small number of corporations control the American economy.

Actually the last statement should be broadened somewhat because many of the leading corporations are best described as multinational conglomerates. This means that such corporations have their business tentacles extended into many countries, and they produce not just one product but many different ones. International Telephone and Telegraph Corporation is a good example. Consistently one of the top fifteen corporations in America, ITT carries on its business in at least forty other countries; and it has been involved in virtually every possible market—not just communications, but also car rentals, consumer finance, insurance, book publishing, etc. As some have pointed out, one could exist as a consumer almost totally within the womb of ITT and not purchase anything from anyone else for one's entire life.

The image of concentration in the American economy intensifies when the board of directors of the major corporations are examined. According to Miller,

> Today, when support is growing for the idea that a board of directors should be an independent source of counsel to a corporation, a Senate study indicates that virtually all of America's most powerful companies are linked together, directly or indirectly, by the men and women who sit on their boards (1978:2).

Conflicts of interest and antitrust illegalities are, of course, quite possible with such interlocking directorates. The Senate study referred to above suggested that the concentration in American business via the interlocks is even greater now than it was in 1914, when the federal antitrust legislation was first enacted.

The concentration of wealth and economic power in the corporate world is analogous to the concentration of individual and family wealth in upper-class hands. And, the stock ownership of the upper class allows it to own and control corporate America. How much stock is needed to control the corporations? Most agree that an individual or family needs 5 percent of a company's stock in order to exert control. Under some circumstances, the percentage may dip as low as 1 percent or 2 percent (Zeitlin, 1978:18).

With the above in mind, one can make a strong argument that the top corporations in America are ruled by a relatively few upper-class families. Heilbroner, for example, states that "Among the 150 supercorporations, there are perhaps as many as 1,500 or 2,000 operational top managers, but as few as 200 to 300 families own blocks of stock that ultimately control these corporations" (Heilbroner, 1965:26). Two hundred to 300 families, in the final analysis, control the economy. That is really the uppermost part of the upper class—the super-rich, families with names such as Dupont, Mellon, Rockefeller, Vanderbilt, and Whitney.

The Mellons' stock ownership, for example, includes 21 percent of Alcoa, 18 percent of Gulf Oil, 20 percent of Koppers, and 40 percent of the Mellon National Bank which, in turn, owns the controlling shares of a number of companies. The Mellons are not an isolated example. The Duponts most likely own the controlling shares of General Motors' stock. They owned 44 percent in 1937, the last date for which precise information is available. It is safe to assume that the Duponts' share of GM has not slipped below 5 percent since then. Any such series of examples, of course, must include the Rockefeller name. It is believed that the Rockefellers control three of the seven largest oil companies in the world through their stock ownership. They also control the Chase Manhattan Bank through their large stockholdings. Brother David has been chairman of the board of Chase which, in turn, has the controlling shares in 56 of the largest US corporations. Among them are Eastern Airlines, TWA, Pan American, Sunbeam, Texas Instruments, Sperry Rand, CBS, and National Steel (Hoffman, 1971:14-15).

Does the Upper Class Really Dominate the Economy?

Most Americans refuse to recognize and accept the picture drawn above as true because of their widespread belief that America is the land of opportunity where everyone can succeed. A small and powerful upper class seems to refute this idea. An example of resistance to our analysis is the belief that

American business is really owned by the little guy: the means of production are owned not by a small upper class, but rather by a broad spectrum of little businessmen. Believers in this myth fail ro recognize that the top 200 corporations have a clear majority (60 percent) of all manufacturing assets. Clearly, small businessmen do not own the means of production in the US. Furthermore, most small businesses either go bankrupt or just barely survive, according to the Small Business Administration. Half of all new business enterprises fold during the first two years. The surviving businesses give many of their owners only a small profit. Competing with the big businesses controlled by the upper class is not so easy after all.

A variation on the little guy theme is the role attributed to pension plans. Many workers in America have a percentage of their paychecks put aside in pension plans for retirement. These monies are usually invested in a variety of corporate stocks and bonds. Does this mean that non-upper class people own and control the means of production? Decidedly not. As Anderson (1974:134) argues, pension plans enhance the clout of upper-class owners who are consequently able "to control larger blocks of property with relatively less stock." The reason for this is that ownership of stock is dispersed through pension plans so that it takes a smaller proportion of the stock to control the corporation. Furthermore, ". . . the $70 billion in bank trusts as pensions in the 1967 data end up under the control of the families and individuals whose finance capital controls the banks" (Anderson, 1974:206). This strongly suggests that pension money is largely under the control of the upper class.

Probably the argument most often heard against the position that an upper class owns and controls the American economy is that there has been a managerial revolution (Berle and Means, 1967). Instead of capitalist owners controlling the corporations, there is a new breed of talented managers who have risen through the corporations because of merit and who make the "important" decisions on the basis of bureaucratic efficiency. A number of clarifying points need to be made here. First of all, the role of managers is not at all antithetical to the interests of upper-class owners of corporations. In fact, their main function is to carry out the established rules of the monopoly game that is American business: protect Boardwalk and Park Place; maximize profits. Indeed, it may be nice to have "hired hands" carry out the dirty work and get the ulcers while the super-rich, the top wealth-owning families, can devote themselves to more leisurely activities, if they so desire.

Also important is that the most powerful managers and the super-rich families are but two different echelons of the upper class. Our basis for saying this is that the income and wealth levels of top management personnel locate them within the upper class as we have defined it. Their stock ownership via stock options is considerable, and consequently their net worth places them within the top 0.5 percent of the wealth distribution. Furthermore, their incomes are substantially above $85,000. It is most accurate to say that the highest ranking managers are in the upper class but at a lower echelon than the super-rich.

So, in reality, the managerial revolution argument comes down to the question of whether the highest echelon of the upper class, the super-rich, or a lower echelon of the upper class, the top managers, controls the corporations the most. Heilbroner's estimate that 200 to 300 upper-class families own the stock that ultimately controls the leading corporations leads to the conclusion that the answer is the highest echelon of the upper class. Or, in the words of Zeitlin, ". . . there are real controlling owners in most if not all of the large corporations that now appear to be under so-called management control" (Zeitlin, 1978:19). Those owners are the first families of the American upper class—the super-rich.

THE POWER OF THE UPPER CLASS

A concentration of power parallels the concentration of wealth and income in upper-class America. Whether it be in terms of upper class families themselves or in terms of the corporations controlled by upper class families, the political institution is best understood as a vehicle for realizing upper-class interests.

Probably the best known articulation of the above argument by an American social scientist is the power elite thesis of C. Wright Mills (1956). Mills located the concentration of power in the top personnel of the big corporations, the executive branch of the federal government, and the military. Among other things, the decisions made by this group "determine the size and shape of the national economy, the level of employment, the purchasing power of the consumer, the prices that are advertised, the investments that are channeled" (Mills, 1956: 125). The few at the top of the economic system, the political system, and the military were interlocked in a variety of ways and ran America according to Mills's analysis. But, of these three areas, the key one was the economic; for example, the rulers of the big corporations shaped the political system.

Following in the tradition of Mills, G. William Domhoff has written a number of books dealing with how the American upper class dominates the political institution. In *Who Rules America?*, Domhoff (1967) documents the existence of a socially cohesive national upper class that owns and controls the corporations. He then proceeds to show how the upper class influences political opinion through its foundations (the Ford and Rockefeller foundations, for example) and its associations such as the Council on Foreign Relations, the Committee for Economic Development, and the National Association of Manufacturers. Upper-class impact upon the federal government is explored through such mechanisms as the financing of the major political parties. The influence of the upper class on such governmental institutions as the CIA and the FBI is also examined.

In *The Higher Circles*, Domhoff (1970) discusses how the upper class rules the national government in both domestic policy and foreign policy. Particularly devastating is Domhoff's analysis of how social legislation has been shaped by the upper class. Usually reforms such as workmen's compensation and social security are interpreted as victories of the organized labor movement. Domhoff's analysis, however, points in another direction. For example, "There is only one group that did not play a key role in the fight for protective labor legislation, and that is organized labor itself" (Domhoff, 1970:177). Rather, upper-class organizations such as the AALL (American Association for Labor Legislation) were behind the reforms. Domhoff posits that the reforms were suggested by the more politically liberal faction of the upper class in order to head off more serious and legitimate demands by the laboring class. Its plan amounted to keeping the masses happy by giving them a few crumbs.

That the upper class is not monolithic in its political ideology needs development. Upper-class people are not all conservative. Some are more progressive in their political orientation than others. Initially, this startles one until the bottom line of protecting upper-class interests is drawn. In this vein, Domhoff explains the seeming diversity of upper-class planning organizations during the 1930s:

> However, from a larger perspective, looking down at the foci of power withing the overall system, these differences were primarily technical conflicts within the power elite over means to agreed ends, those ends being the maintenance of the wealth distribution and a private property system in which a very small percentage of the population enjoys a great prestige, privilege and authority (1970: 185).

The above pattern still exists today. This is illustrated by the upper class role in political campaign funding. Upper class influence in the Republican party hardly needs mention. What comes as a more of a surprise is that the Democratic party, usually considered to be the party of the workingman, is also so influenced albeit to a lesser extent (Domhoff, 1972). So, *both* major political parties are influenced by the upper class.

Another example of the upper class covering a variety of different parts of the political spectrum that are acceptable is that in 1972 Gulf, the Mellons' oil company, gave contributions both to the Republican candidate for the presidency, Nixon, and at least two potential Democratic candidates for the same office, Senators Henry Jackson and Wilbur Mills. True enough, Nixon received $100,000, whereas Mills and Jackson got $15,000 and $10,000 respectively; but the point is clear that Gulf did not intend to be left out in the cold. Upper class individuals such as Howard Hughes have privately done the same thing as the Gulf Corporation: that is, contribute to both of the major political parties, not only at the federal level of government but also at the state and local levels.

The effect of these instances is that it is virtually impossible for a serious candidate for major political office in America to be elected without being beholden to upper-class interests in a significant way. Once again, the reason for this is that not only the Republican party but also the Democratic party is heavily affected by the upper class. In fact, there has never been a major political party in the US that has seriously questioned corporate capitalism—the economic system that benefits the upper class. A major reason for this is that any such political party would have a difficult time surviving without upper-class support.

Objections to the Power Elite Thesis

The interpretation that the upper class controls the political institution meets wth strong opposition from many quarters: What about the right of everyone to vote? Does that not put the non-upper class in the dominant position? There is a potential power in the non-upper class vote, but it remains unrealized. A major reason for it remaining unrealized is that there are many divisions within the non-upper class—racial and religious among others—which divert attention away from upper class domination. Chapter 4 explores the impact of these divisions in greater detail.

A further question about the power of the vote argument is that if, in fact, the major political candidates are all in line with upper class interests, why vote? As some would argue, "Either way you choose, you lose." In this context, the low voter turnout of about 50 percent on recent presidential election days may be interpreted as a realistic appraisal of the alternatives offered—namely, very little or none at all.

A variation on the power of the vote argument is that public opinion is crucial and helps to determine national policy. There is no question that in very lopsided situations public opinion can be effective, but, on balance, it appears to be relatively unimportant for the making of important decisions in American political life (Domhoff, 1970:148-153). Also, it should not be overlooked that public opinion can be manipulated. Roszak offers an example concerning US involvement in Vietnam:

Thus, if 80 percent think it is a "mistake" that we ever "went into" Vietnam, but 51 percent think that we would "lose prestige" if we "pulled out now," then the "people" have been "consulted" and the war goes on with their "approval" (1969:16).

Many who deny that the upper class controls the political institution assert that pluralism, instead, characterizes the organization of power in American politics. In other words, American life has many centers of power in big business, in big labor, among consumers, farmers, and others, which vie with one another and counter-balance one another by a system of checks and balances. Mills' (1956) response to this is that pluralism may adequately explain some of what goes on at the lower levels of power; but, on the other hand, the critical decisions about the economy and foreign policy are still made by the highest echelon of the power structure, the power elite.

An example of a new locus of power in America exaggerated by pluralists is the role of technical experts who create research results that are important for big decisions. Aren't they coequal with power elite decision makers? Domhoff argues to the contrary: "It is the function of the decision-maker to choose among the usually conflicting advice that he receives from his usually divided experts" (Domhoff, 1967:149). The advice chosen, one surmises, is that which least threatens the interests of the upper class, especially the private property sytem.

Further Evidence of Upper-Class Power

If we look at contemporary America, we see plainly a plethora of evidence supporting the argument that the upper class dominates the political institution as well as the economic institution. Let us look at the political clout of some super-rich families.

The DuPonts have virtually controlled Delaware politics at all levels. Nader and Green describe the extent to which this is true:

The recent county executive was a former DuPont lawyer, the father of Wilmingon's past mayor was a prominent DuPont executive. The state's one congressman is Pierre S. DuPont IV; its attorney-general is married to a DuPont and is the son of a DuPont executive;

the recent governor, Russell Peterson, was a former DuPont research director. People connected with the firm or the family comprise a fourth of the state legislature, a third of its committee heads, the president pro tempore of the Senate, and the majority leader of the Delaware House (1973:38).

The DuPonts also employed 11 percent of the work force and manufactured 20 percent of the gross product of Delaware. Furthermore, they owned the company responsible for the two largest newspapers, and they controlled the largest bank in the state. Domination on a large scale, one might say.

Rockefeller influence on national political life is well known through the lifetime career of Nelson Rockefeller. And, of course, other Rockefellers have been and are governors of different states. More interesting perhaps is the story of David Rockefeller who has resisted direct participation in the political arena. Why? So powerful has been David's position as chairman of the board at Chase Manhattan that, according to Hoffman, ". . . the presidency of the United States would be a demotion" (Hoffman, 1971:12). For David Rockefeller it seems more efficient to infuence who will run the government while devoting full time attention to business. Serving the purpose of preparing government personnel has been his creation, the Trilateral Commission. This is a study group of leading industrialists and financiers from the United States, Western Europe, and Japan who share ideas on how the world ought to be run. Past members of the commission include former President Carter and eighteen top executives in his administration. Among them have been the Secretaries of Defense, State, and Treasury. Also, Carter's national security adviser, Zbigniew Brzezinski, was formerly the director of the commission.

Other examples of particular upper-class families dominating the political process can be cited. The focus now shifts, however, to a number of trends that show the overall pattern of upper-class power. To be discussed are: (1) political campaign funding; (2) the flow of personnel between government and big business; (3) government regulatory agencies; and (4) government subsidization of the upper class and its big businesses.

Everybody knows that it takes a lot of money to be elected

to high political office today. Most, however, would be surprised to know the extent to which this is true. Approximately a third of the US Senate is comprised of men who are millionaires. On the other hand, one can literally count on one hand how many members of the entire Congress have come directly from the blue-collar world. Obviously, the expense of running for political office puts candidates from the upper class at a distinct advantage.

In a similar way, upper-class influence can once again be seen in the area of campaign contributions. Domhoff (1970:337) indicates that one percent of the population has been responsible for 90 percent of the funding for federal campaigns. It's not difficult to infer the role of the upper class here. A glaring example of this pattern is that insurance tycoon W. Clement Stone gave four million dollars to Nixon's campaigns of 1968 and 1972. Nixon spent 62 million dollars on his 1972 campaign. It does not take an intellectual giant to figure out that something is expected in return for such support. In the case of Stone, an offer of an ambassadorship was made. In general, the political campaign contributions of the upper class insure that business interests will be realized in the political process.

Campaign reform legislation passed in 1974 has somewhat lessened the ability of the upper class to "buy" elections because limitations have been put on how much money a person can contribute to a particular presidential candidate. Public financing of presidential elections has also become a reality. All of the evidence is not yet in on how effective this legislation has been. Preliminary evidence suggests that upper-class people, while not cutting off contributions to presidential candidates, may have given more of their money to congressional candidates in 1976 because public financing of congressional elections wasn't a reality.

The upper class also dominates the political process by making sure that there is a favorable flow of personnel back and forth between big business and big government—a flow that will benefit the big businesses which are owned and controlled by the upper class. We have already cited the example of the Carter Administration where eighteen top executives formerly were members of the heavily business-influenced

Trilateral Commission. One of these, Secretary of Treasury Blumenthal, previously headed the Bendix Corporation. Secretary of Treasury Miller, the second person to hold the post under President Carter, came to government work after being the chairman of Textron, Inc. This linkage between big business and high government office is not unique to the Carter Administration. Key government positions have always been manned by business leaders. Recent secretaries of defense, for example, have been recruited from the top executive positions at General Motors (Wilson) and Ford (McNamara). Typical of the pattern of big business influence that we are suggesting is the statement made by Wilson that "What's good for GM is good for America," rather than the reverse.

The flow of personnel from business to government is best illustrated in the cases where business executives move into government positions whose purpose is to regulate the business that they have left. An example from not too long ago is Earl Butz who moved from the top of Ralston-Purina, a leading food producer, to his position as secretary of agriculture. This pattern is duplicated over and over again in the government regulatory agencies, such as the Federal Power Commission, the Interstate Commerce Commission, the Federal Trade Commission, and the Federal Energy Administration, which have the job of overseeing particular industries. Appointments to these regulatory groups are very much determined by the business concerned. In fact, a not uncommon path for upward mobility within the corporation has been to take a leave of absence from the corporation and move to a government regulation position for a minimal salary, in some instances, a dollar a year, while still getting paid a hefty executive salary by the corporation. After a tour of duty with the regulatory group, where one has been regulating himself or herself, one returns to the corporation at a higher position.

Governmental regulatory groups concerned with setting the national energy policy have been prime examples of the tendency for self-regulation. The men in the top positions, for example, the Federal Energy Administration (now converted to the Department of Energy) and the Federal Power Commission, clearly have had the interest of Big Oil in mind rather than the interests of the public (Anderson and Whitten, 1977). Also, such a trend is not restricted to government at the federal level. When its interests are threatened, Big Business also seeks to control the regulatory groups at the lower levels of government. For instance, Hill (1970) reported that most state anti-pollution boards are filled with people who come from the corporations responsible for the pollution.

A final point needs to be made about the flow of personnel between government and business. Business interests are obviously met when the flow is from business to government. The reverse is also true. When one leaves a government position, a step often taken is to move into a Big Business executive job. Clark MacGregor, for example, went from a top position in the Nixon administration to the vice-presidency of United Aircraft. Or, more recently, we see Alexander Haig moving from the position of NATO commander to the presidency of United Technologies, a major defense contractor. Obviously, the ex-government worker can act as a liaison between the corporation and the government for lobbying purposes.

So, what is the payoff that the upper class receives as a result of its obvious political power? It is easy to oversimplify and keep reiterating that business interests are met as a result of upper-class clout. More needs to be said, however, about government subsidization of the upper class, or socialism for the rich as it is sometimes called.

Turner and Starnes (1967:89) describe the bonanza gained by the upper class and its big businesses as part of a governmental wealthfare system consisting of: (1) governmental purchases, (2) governmental price supports, (3) export-import programs, and (4) government taxation policies. Government purchases are exemplified by the huge defense contracts given to many major corporations. (In 1974 the Defense Department spent $165,000 every minute of every hour of every day.) The benefit of price support systems and export-import programs to the upper class is that both make sure that the profits of the corporations are protected and kept high.

It has already been seen that tax legislation has been set up for the distinct advantage of upper-class people. As W. Clement Stone suggests, "If income taxes were 99 percent, we'd find a way." Similar legislation benefits the large corporations. Theoretically, there is a federal tax on corporate income of 48 percent. But we find out that corporations like Ford in 1975 and 1976 indeed do have a better idea: they pay no taxes. Ford is not alone; in 1977 U.S. Steel, Eastern Airlines, and the Chase Manhattan Corporation, among others, paid no taxes.

How can they avoid taxes? For our answer we return to the tax loopholes, for example, exclusions and deductions from gross income, tax credits, and special tax rates. Why do the tax loopholes exist? Upper-class influence is the obvious answer as can be seen in the remarks of Senator Kennedy:

> The shameful fact is that many of these special provisions have no merit at all. They are insinuated into the tax bills at the behest of lobbyists and added at the request of big campaign contributors. It gives the obvious impression that the Internal Revenue Code is up for sale (TRB, 1976:7).

The same reasoning can be applied to why the upper class and its big businesses receive the other benefits listed by Turner and Starnes in the government wealthfare system which they outline. And in the background we still hear the plaintive prayer of the non-upper class continue: "Let us be a gigantic corporation so that we may plow all our income back into developing ourselves and owe only $18.63 in tax" (Baker, 1977:12).

IMPLICATIONS FOR CHANGE

The upper class owns and controls the economic system; it dominates the political institution. Non-upper class America is largely unconscious of both facts. When it shows glimmers of recognition on either of these scores, a number of reflex, and reactive statements are made: "Well, we need them for our jobs"; or "You can't fight city hall"; or "They've got the guns." These are hard statements to refute persuasively when one realizes the extent to which most Americans are caught up in the necessary rat race of day-to-day survival. There are other obstacles to doing anything about the status quo which must be considered before it makes sense to discuss the options open to the non-upper class. The next three chapters will involve a consideration of what some of the other obstacles are. A discussion of alternative paths of reaction to upper-class domination of America will then be in order.

THE AMERICAN CULTURE AND
THE REALITY OF CLASS STRATIFICATION

The facts of inequality in America are very disturbing. How do Americans rationalize such tremendous concentration of power and wealth? A major part of the answer can be found in the traditional American culture which praises individual success, diverts attention from class stratification, and locates blame for the excesses of inequality in nonthreatening places.

THE AMERICAN CULTURE AND STRATIFICATION

The American Dream Package

A core part of the culture is the American Dream Package— a set of values, beliefs, and rationalization which defend the existing stratification system. Included are the approval of equality of opportunity, individualism, competition, hard work, deferred gratification, social mobility, and success.

The belief in equal opportunity conveys the notion that everyone should be able to have an equal chance to get ahead, achieve, and be successful. This does not mean that most Americans believe that everyone actually should be equal in what they earn, own, and possess: that is, enjoy equality of condition. Indeed, it is more typical for Americans to think that people should be rewarded according to what they do or produce. Both this phenomenon and other aspects of the American Dream Package have been explored by a variety of scholars.

Such disparate social analysts as Williams (1970) and Slater

(1976) have observed that individualism is at the heart of the traditional American culture. Each person ultimately is responsible for the development and growth of his or her own life. What one makes of one's equal opportunity to succeed depends upon what the individual does with his or her chances. This means that one must be competitive if one is to maximize personal achievement and success. The traditional American culture views the world as being a Darwinian jungle where survival of the fittest is the rule. Analysts like Slater (1976) suggest that this competition is heavily laced with Oedipal striving. This view of competition gives an interesting motive to the pursuit of upward social mobility: outdo the parent of the same sex by improving upon one's initial family stratification position. We may be number two, but like Avis we try harder.

Regardless of whether or not the motivation is conscious or unconscious, upward social mobility has been held up as a goal ever since America began to serve as a land of opportunity for the first European settlers. Rags to riches mobility is to be accomplished by hard work according to the work ethic. If a person works hard, he or she can go as far as desired because the opportunities for success are there. Survey results (Rytina, Form, and Pease, 1970) indicate that both rich and non-rich Americans today still hold the same beliefs. Of course, the culture does not say that upward mobility will be easy. One is supposed to defer gratification—or sacrifice now for future satisfaction—along the way. Staying in school for a longer period of time or delaying marriage until later ages are often pointed to as examples of deferring gratification. Once upward social mobility has been achieved, personal success has been achieved. The two are as one. Then, the traditional American culture encourages one to demonstrate the achievement of personal success by the consumption and display of material possessions that signify the status of success. Prestigious cars and homes, luxurious vacations, and leisurely pursuits are the appropriate grist here. Also, the consumption behavior of the successful usually determines what is considered "in" or "trendy" by most Americans.

Closely related to the foregoing is the belief held by many

that most Americans have done well by the American Dream Package. This is exemplified by the conviction that America has a large "middle class" predominantly made up of white-collar workers. Such people have "made it" and enjoy a very comfortable, affluent existence, so the stereotype goes. This tends to reinforce the belief in equality of opportunity for all people and in the rest of the American Dream Package. The "system" works.

Blaming the Individual

The system works, but many people, if not most, in America are upset with the stratification position that they personally "achieve." A sense of frustration develops because one has not gone further in the structure, that is, experienced rags-to-riches mobility. Who is one to blame: the upper class; the poor; the individual person?

Let us consider the last option first, namely, the individual person as scapegoat. The individual person who is upset with his or her stratification position is encouraged by the culture's emphasis upon individualism and equality of opportunity to blame the self for not achieving more success. "It's my own fault. If I'd tried harder and had more stick-to-itive-ness, I'd have gone further. I wouldn't be where I am today," reason many individuals. How often do we hear the above or some variation said explicitly or implicitly? A garbage man from a study by Sennett and Cobb speaks:

> "Look, I know it's nobody's fault but mine that I got stuck here where I am, I mean . . . if I wasn't such a dumb shit . . . no, it ain't that neither . . . if I'd applied myself, I know I got it in me to be different, can't say anyone did it to me" (1972:96).

Self-blaming for not going further in the stratification system has been a part of America's cultural baggage since the first European immigrants sought this fabled land of opportunity. The opportunity is there for those who want it. Those who do not take advantage of it have only themselves to blame. The open frontier of the West was especially interesting in this light. If one had a low stratification position in the East, one could always go West and start over again in an attempt to leap from rags to riches. Of course, most of those who tried this did not improve their situation much, but how could they complain? Now they had failed gain. It was their own fault. Self-blaming was reinforced.

Lewis (1978) characterizes the rationalizations and behavior cited above as reflecting what he calls the "individual-as-central-sensibility." The fruits of inequality are not caused by some "system" or "structure" out there; rather, the blame is to be found rooted in the actions of individual people who are responsible for their positions in the stratification system. Such lines of reasoning are familiar to the ears of most of us. Indeed, they are a part of the official wisdom.

It is important to note also that individuals who blame themselves for not going further in the stratification system do develop a variety of mental defenses. These defenses can minimize the sting of self-blame by covering up the gap between real achievement and imagined opportunities. As research dating back to that done by the Lynds has shown, a very important mental defense has been to think less and less of one's own stratification position and refocus attention upon the social mobility chances open to one's children. Such mobility can be shared vicariously by the parents and hence serve to make partial sense out of their own stratification position. Unfortunately, there is often a tragic underside to this scenario. The children in such families often suffer from the resulting pressure upon them and wind up resenting it. Even more poignant, however, is the fact that the parents of these families frequently tell their children either explicitly or implicitly not to be like them because they are failures. As Sennett and Cobb (1972) have indicated, such parents view themselves not as models for their kids but as warnings of what could happen to them if they do not become successful.

As the research of Chinoy (1955) and others shows, another means of coping with the self-blaming dilemma is to consume status items that represent success even though one has not directly experienced the success of social mobility. This means that one can fail to acquire some important elements of the American Dream Package and still try to share in its ultimate rewards by buying the right material possessions. The automobile industry provides a good example. One can buy a moderately priced, large car that looks like a Mercedes (and therefore signifies success) for slightly more money than one pays for an "economical" subcompact car. It is no secret that Detroit has been trying to sell the average white-collar worker such cars by promising them the psychological sense of success in its advertising. There is much evidence of the efficacy of "success" advertising for many consumer products. The ultimate role of the resultant consumption is to divert attention away from the fact that people haven't really been as successful in the stratification system as they had hoped. It does this by making them *feel* like they actually have been successful. Of course, there are other escape valves for one's frustrations besides the consumption and display of the appropriate material objects.

Blaming the Poor

Enter the poor. People in the white-collar and blue-collar worlds, who have not gone as far in the stratification system as the American Dream Package tells them they should have gone, can also draw significant comfort from the fact that a relatively large group of poor people have not achieved as much as they have. This tends to inflate the stratification position of the non-poor. The following line of reasoning is typical of this attitude: "I may not have gone as far as I could have gone, but at least I've accomplished more than these people."

Why are the poor in their position? Many assume the stratification position of the poor to be the result of their not bothering to open up the American Dream Package containing the opportunity for social mobility and success. They blame the poor for not taking advantage of the opportunities available to all. They view the poor as failures because of their laziness, shiftlessness, and immorality. Such negative interpretations of the poor have been characteristic of the traditional American culture throughout our history.

Most Americans have assimilated the traditional culture well and are very adept, in the words of Ryan (1976), at "blaming the victim": The poor have bad housing because they do not take care of it, rather than the poor have little money for housing. The poor don't do well in school because they do not try to learn, rather than the poor don't succeed in school because there is inadequate funding for their schooling. In the above cases, the poor are victims who are blamed for their difficulties. The "system," the social structure, and upper-class America are not blamed.

Blaming the poor does not stop with blaming them for their own situation. The poor also are blamed for the frustrations felt by white-collar and blue-collar people. Perhaps the most glaring example of how the poor serve this function is illustrated by the following reasoning: "Most of the poor are on welfare. Most people on welfare are chiselers." Both statements are false, but they are more than obliquely implied when we hear frustrated folks in the middle of the stratification system say, "I had to work for what I've got." Such sentiments are played upon when newspapers place the telephone number of the welfare office on their front pages with the accompanying suggestion that anyone knowing of a welfare chiseler should call the number and inform the authorities. Similarly, the 1972 Nixon re-election campaign ran a televison ad where a person was shown walking to the welfare office. An ominous background voice informed a construction worker that it was his tax dollars that were subsidizing the welfare recipient. As we indicated in Chapter 2, many white-collar and blue-collar individuals have to stretch each of their dollars in order to survive from paycheck to paycheck. High taxes contribute to the squeeze that they are in. Following the logic of the Nixon commercial, many blame the poor for part of the squeeze because, "It's my tax dollars that are supporting the welfare chiseler." One result of this thinking is that the non-upper class is severely fragmented.

Another way in which the poor are blamed for frustrations felt by blue-collar and white-collar Americans is related to crime, one of the prime concerns of many. Crime is identified with "crime in the streets" which, in turn, is equated with crimes committed by poor people, especially poor blacks. This is important for two reasons. First, the poor once again provide a favorable frame of comparison for people in the middle of the stratification system. They can feel good about themselves by saying, "Well, at least I haven't sunk that low." Secondly, crime is seen as something that poor people do. Poor people are blamed for most crimes. Attention is shifted away from white-collar crime, or "crime in the suites." There is no question that the upper-class dominated media play a critical role in perpetuating this interpretation of crime. Upper-class crime, for example, is rarely considered to be front-page material. As a result, people in the middle tend to blame the poor for one of their biggest worries—crime. This fits the overall pattern where those in white-collar and blue-collar America are encouraged by the traditional American culture to point the finger of blame downstairs at the poor rather than to look upstairs at the upper class for the source of their frustrations.

Blaming the Upper Class

In order to discuss the question of whether or not the upper class is blamed for the frustrations felt by non-upper class people, one should point out that not all non-upper class Americans perceive the existence of a small, wealthy upper class. Indeed, for some, a spin-off of the belief in a large, comfortable "middle class" is the corollary belief that an upper class as we have described it does not really exist; or if it does, it is not that much better off than the "middle class." America may not necessarily be classless, but there has been dispersal of the ownership of the means of production throughout a broad segment of the population, so this rationale argues. And furthermore, there may be some very rich people in America, but they really get clobbered by the tax structure.

We will save more specific responses to this mindset until we discuss the reality of stratification in detail. We will only indicate here that, as we have argued in Chapter 2, the upper class does own and control the means of production in the United States. Why, then, is not the upper class blamed for the stratification frustrations felt by non-upper class people? It is not possible to precisely rank the reasons because so little empirical research has been done on the non-upper class view of the upper class, an interesting point in and of itself. Nevertheless, the following reasons seem to be important for those non-upper class people who do actually perceive the existence of an upper class in America.

A belief held by some is that upper-class people deserve their position because they have worked hard to earn it. They have opened up the American Dream Package correctly. They have followed the rules of the game, so naturally they are where they should be. Furthermore, they are models for the rest of us to follow rather than blame. An approximate sociological rendition of this argument is the functional argument for the existence of stratification (Davis and Moore, 1945). Loosely translated, the functional argument states that stratification is a reward system designed to motivate people to work hard. It pays off those who do work hard and get to the top. Such arguments and beliefs, however, overlook the fact that most large incomes in America are based upon the inheritance of unearned income sources (Lundberg, 1968). Such knowledge, though, is not part of the conventional wisdom. Rather, Horatio Alger rags-to-riches stories are presented to the non-upper class by a variety of upper-class dominated institutions.

Another interpretation of the upper class is that it provides the non-upper class with a fantasy world. Non-upper class members can vicariously enjoy the life-style of the more visible segments of the upper class. One can see ample evidence of this in contemporary society. The "people" sections of newspapers and television news programs draw heavily upon this "reality" by keeping us aware of the latest doings of a variety of upper-class members. Similarly, if one goes on guided tours of major metropolitan areas, notable upper-class homes are always singled out to a chorus of *oohs* and *aahs* from those on the tour. Tours of the homes of the rich also attest to the admiration that many non-upper class Americans feel for the upper class. Of course, positive feelings towards the upper class are not always evoked by the examples cited above. This is especially the case when one hears of the extravagances of some of the rich (for example, parties in Newport, Rhode Island, where cigarettes for guests have been rolled in one hundred dollar bills). Nevertheless, on balance, the fantasy world created by the upper class encourages the non-upper class to identify with them rather than blame them.

On the other hand, negative feelings are engendered by the

knowledge that a significant number of upper-class people have skirted the edges of propriety in order to attain their position. America, for example, has a rich tradition of robber barons— Carnegie, Frick, Harriman, Mellon, and Rockefeller, for example—who essentially swindled their way to incredible wealth. Indeed, Slater (1976:42) asserts that most great fortunes in America have been made this way. The truth of this statement upsets members of the non-upper class. Also, it would seem to lead many to a stance of blaming the rich rather than the poor and cause them to want to fight for change in the existing distribution of wealth and power. Such is not necessarily the case, however, as a number of further rationalizations attest. For example, some argue that even if upper-class wealth originated in some illegalities, one cannot blame the heirs of the robber barons, since they have only inherited their position.

Some members of the non-upper class also defend upper-class people by praising them for their philanthropy. They feel that the rich give their wealth away to charitable causes from which non-upper class people benefit. A popular show on television, "The Millionaire," dramatized this point by having an anonymous millionaire give out a million dollars to some needy soul each week. It should be pointed out that upper-class philanthropy is rarely given to causes that might severely question or threaten the political and economic status quo. (An exception to this is one of the Pillsbury heirs who has been known to give money to somewhat radical causes and thereby has the nickname of the "Doughboy.") Indeed, a considerable amount of so-called philanthropy is not only a means of defending and maintaining the position of the upper class but also a tax write-off to boot. As a prime example, Nicholas von Hoffman notes that "Hughes' only charity, the Howard Hughes Medical Institute, was a philanthropic fraud whereby the tax laws were manipulated to keep the tycoon yet richer and more powerful" (von Hoffman, 1979:21).

There are other negative interpretations of the upper class which do not usually lead non-upper class people to blame the upper class for their frustrations. Some still have a religious rationale that says the upper class is not to be envied because an abundance of money leads to temptations which make it difficult to lead a good life. "It is easier for a camel to pass through the eye of a needle, than for a rich man to enter the kingdom of God" (St. Mark: Chapter 10).

Somewhat similar to negative moral interpretations of the rich are rationalizations pointing to the psychological and character defects which seem to flow from possessing a lot of money. Examples confirming these suspicions abound. J. Paul Getty once again provides us with illustrations of these points. It seems more than a bit odd that a man of his wealth would have a public telephone installed in one of his homes. Getty did this in order to avoid having people make calls on his private telephone that would have cost him money. Getty also had one of his homes decorated in the style and mode of ancient Rome because he thought that he was the reincarnation of the emperor Hadrian. Howard Hughes, of course, barely needs mention in this context. Most have already heard of his bizarre, reclusive life and the way in which he let his body decay and become dependent upon drugs. And the list of upper-class people with similar horror stories could go on and on. Obviously, though, not all upper-class people suffer severe mental difficulties. In fact, they have the opportunity to enjoy life and have good mental health more than anyone else. The belief that upper-class wealth brings special problems, however, probably does serve to comfort some non-upper class people about their own difficulties.

A final defense of the upper class by the non-upper class is the reasoning that the upper class, because of its position, can and does help the rest of the population in ways other than philanthropy. For example, it can provide political leadership. As we saw in Chapter 2, the upper class does play a significant role in the political process, but it seems clear that this role is one of either protecting or furthering upper-class interests rather than non-upper class interests. A similar rationalization holds that the upper class helps the non-upper class by providing it with jobs in the corporations that the upper class owns and controls. This is a version of the formula that business success ultimately means success for all—via a gradual trickle-down effect. Such a rationale also usually includes the belief that if anything is done to upset upper-class people (for example, changing tax laws that currently favor them), they can take their money out of certain business ventures which, in turn, will mean the end of jobs for average non-upper class people. While this is potentially true to some degree, a fundamental question to ask is why the upper class is allowed to own the corporations in the first place. Why is it allowed to have such a stranglehold over the economy and, as a result, the rest of the population?

By the way of summary, some of the rationalizations discussed above defend the position of the upper class in America. For example, parts of the non-upper class believe that the upper class has earned its position and deserves it, and that the upper class provides the non-upper class with jobs, material for fantasies, political leadership, and charitable contributions. Such lines of reasoning encourage non-upper class people to admire the upper class and, perhaps, to model themselves after the upper class. "Work hard, become successful, and you can become part of the upper class yourself," is an opinion voiced by quite a few members of the non-upper class. Certainly such arguments do not lead many into a position of wanting to blame or challenge the upper class. Other rationales considered above take a more negative view of upper-class people by emphasizing their *faux pas* such as the bizarre behavior often attributed to them. Such beliefs probably have the effect of making non-upper class people more accepting of their own fate because the advantages of the upper class are seen as not worth the consequent troubles. Finally, there also are interpretations of upper-class people that show resentment. These views see them as extravagant robber barons who exploit the working man. There is no doubt that many Americans harbor such thoughts that, indeed, do blame the upper class. That there is not more blaming of the upper class that gets openly and politically expressed is surprising.

Cultural Obstacles of a Political Nature

Even for those who do blame the upper class, the American cultural system contains a number of political beliefs and values which make it difficult to translate any such blame into political action. This is because the upper-class dominated stratification system is propped up by certain political values through which any blame must be filtered.

Crucial to the political part of the culture is the belief in patriotism or love of country which many have maintained even though Viet Nam and Watergate have tarnished it somewhat. To blame the rich and carry out that blame into political action violates patriotism for many: The upper class *is* the American Dream, even if some upper-class members have not earned their position honestly. Therefore, to challenge the upper class is unpatriotic. On the other hand, to blame the poor and carry out that blame into the political arena is allowable because the poor represent what is worst about America: They haven't opened up the American Dream Package. Patriotism is also important in this context because to blame the upper class and to act accordingly in a political way is to question the existing stratification position of the upper class. This means challenging the political staus quo and challenging the status quo is often viewed as unpatriotic.

Another political value worthy of mention here is nationalism: that is, putting national interests first which, for many, flows out of patriotism. Nationalism creates a safety valve for those upset with internal stratification because it fosters negative feelings about foreign countries and peoples that, in turn, become scapegoats for the frustrations about inequality in the homeland. Nationalism and patriotism can also encourage non-upper class Americans to compare their position with that of non-upper class people in other countries—especially third world countries—rather than with the American upper class. To do the former instead of the latter can lead one to a more resigned feeling about the concentration of wealth and power within the United States.

Finally, it is difficult to implement politically any desire to blame the upper class because of our belief in democracy, or government for the people and by the people. Many believe that our democratic institutions, such as the universal right to vote, have delivered the goods for the great mass of the population— the non-upper class. This makes content some non-upper class members who might otherwise be tempted to fight for change in the existing stratification system.

Of course, even those who do not buy any of the values and beliefs discussed so far face major obstacles. Aside from demanding a substantial amount of money, getting political change in America requires a lot of time and energy. When this political reality is coupled with the fact that most non-upper class people have little time or energy left over after trying to survive their nine-to-five workdays, it is easier to see why more blaming of the upper class is not openly expressed. An attitude of fatalistic acceptance ("You can't fight city hall") can readily follow. But, it doesn't have to be this way.

Status versus Class

Our consideration of traditional American culture concludes with a subtle, yet significant, point discussed in Chapter 1. The value system emphasizes status differences within the non-upper class (the white-collar world, the blue-collar world, and the poor) more so than the class difference between the upper class and the non-upper class. In short, status position is stressed more than class position.

People focus on different things depending upon whether class or status is viewed as most pivotal. Class position is one's economic position (that is, one's relation to the means of production). Status, on the other hand, is equivalent with prestige. While class position influences status position, other factors related to status such as style of life, taste, and occupational role are more salient in American society.

The role of status in America can be seen in relationship to the American Dream Package values of success and the consumption of material possessions symbolizing success. As mentioned previously, one can short-circuit the American Dream Package by trying to buy the appropriate material possessions even if success has not been achieved. In so doing, one can seek the status of those who are successful: to buy material possessions like those of the successful is to buy their style of life and their higher status. Big Business attempts to cash in on this tendency by mass producing and by advertising items thought to convey status. A good example is when what is high fashion in clothing today appears in moderately priced stores tomorrow. Unless one sharpens his or her critical eye, it is difficult to tell the difference between big-name designers' masterpieces and mass-produced goods. As a result, many Americans seek to improve their status by buying the right things; but they just "keep up with the Joneses" because the Joneses are doing the same thing. Furthermore, virtually all non-upper class people who participate in such status-seeking consumption really fail to achieve the elite status of the upper class.

Such status concerns have important effects, however. Because we are involved in status seeking via consumption, our class position in the system of economic production is either forgotten, obscured, or downplayed. In fact, when we do think of our work roles, we think of them more in terms of status (prestige) than class (relationship to the means of production). The culture encourages us to make status comparisons with other workers. A major way that we do this in America is by means of the white-collar versus blue-collar comparison.

White-collar workers have more status than blue-collar workers. Their incomes are higher. They wear "nicer" clothes to work. They get paid a salary, not an hourly wage. They do not have to "punch in" at a certain time every day. They do not have to ask for permission to go to the bathroom while at work as some blue-collar workers must. Also, white-collar workers do not belong to unions as do blue-collar workers. This is because union membership is viewed as a status detraction. (Ironically, more and more white-collar workers are joining unions today and giving up a status advantage over the blue-collar world because it is getting more and more difficult to eat prestige.)

An interesting footnote to this discussion is that the concept of class has been co-opted by the traditional American culture. By co-optation we mean that the concept has been redefined for everyday usage. It is drained of any radical meaning and, on the contrary, made unthreatening and safe. Furthermore, sometimes the newly-defined term of *class* is actually used to promote the products of the traditional culture. To illustrate this point, the concept of class in its strictly sociological meaning (especially in the Marxist tradition) has readily brought forth revolutionary images of class struggle and class conflict. Sociological discussions of "class" also suggest that people have a relatively fixed, permanent position in the economic system. Such meanings do not appear in our every-day usage of the term. Instead, "class" is taken to mean high style in behavior and appearance, precisely what part of status refers to in the more technical sociological interpretation. As a result of this translation, when we say in everyday conversation that someone has "class," we are really saying that they have status. Commercials for a variety of products have used the term of class in this co-opted sense (An advertisement for one beer claims, "It's got class."). Indeed, the concept of class has come a long way.

Status seeking via consumption, white collar/blue collar comparisons, and the co-optation of the term "class" are all examples of how the American culture stresses status more than class. The net effect is that the value system emphasizes awareness of relatively minute status differences within the non-upper class while, at the same time, it blocks consciousness of the gross class difference between the upper class and the non-upper class.

Thus far we have discussed how the American culture stands on stratification related issues. The cornerstone is the American Dream Package which says that individuals should be competitive and work hard so that upward social mobility and success can be achieved. Those who do not "make it" are supposed to blame themselves or the poor but not the upper class. If one does blame the upper class, the political values of patriotism, nationalism, and democracy enter in to defuse much of the political action that could be based upon the blaming of the upper class. Also, the culture promotes status awareness and discourages class consciousness. Finally, all these aspects of the traditional cultural system get perpetuated in America through the institutions of the economy, the political structure, the educational system, religion, and the family.

THE REALITY OF STRATIFICATION

An Overview

What about the reality of stratification in America today? How does it compare with the traditional American cultural system outlined above? Obviously there are both contradictions and agreements between the two; but, on balance, the evidence suggests more contradictions.

A major area of discrepancy between the culture and reality concerns the extent to which class stratification exists. As we noted above, the culture emphasizes status and downplays class. A careful reading of Chapter 2 shows how extreme class stratification actually is in America. The contrast between the upper class and the non-upper class in income, wealth, and control of the economy makes the status stratification between the elite, the white-collar world, the blue-collar world, and the poor seem like mere child's play by comparison. The top of the upper class has astronomically high yearly incomes, while the median family income for the non-upper class in 1975 was under $15,000. The latter figure is less than one half of what it took to start leading a comfortable existence. Obviously, this information challenges the widely held belief that most Americans have an affluent life-style. Also, if we include the reality of those at the very bottom of the non-upper class (the bag ladies, the elderly, and the children who must eat dog food in order to survive), the starkness of the contrast between the top and the bottom of the class stratification system becomes all the more apparent.

That the upper class owns 50 percent of the corporate stocks and bonds in the US shows the impact of class. Such concentration violates the belief that the ownership of the means of production has been dispersed through a large segment of the American population. In reality, very few non-upper class people "Own a piece of the rock"; this is attested by the fact that in 1969 the net worth of 75 percent of the population was $10,000 or less. A majority of the population owned virtually nothing, much less the means of production.

The facts of class stratification also contradict the rationalization that the upper class has earned its position. As indicated previously, most large incomes in America are based upon the inheritance of unearned income sources. Earning one's position by playing out the American Dream Package and experiencing rags to riches social mobility hardly characterizes the situation of most upper-class Americans. Another belief about upper-class people is that they may have high incomes, but at least they have to pay high taxes by virtue of the system of progressive taxation in the United States. In reality, most US taxation is either directly regressive, such as the Social Security tax, or it is indirectly regressive by means of a system of tax loopholes. The ultimate reality is that a J. Paul Getty can pay the same yearly tax as the average family that earns the median income.

Tax laws, of course, are determined by who has political power. This leads to another example related to the contrast between the traditional culture and the reality of class stratification. Americans believe in democracy—that all should have a say in the political process. However, as Chpater 2 points out, the class position of the upper class is translated by a number of means into inordinate political power. To call the upper class a ruling class is not an exaggeration. Its effect is to make our belief in political democracy difficult, if not impossible, to implement.

Difficulties in the American Perception of Stratification

Much stratification research dating back to the Lynds' studies of Middletown documents the failure of Americans to recognize the severity of stratification in America. Indeed, many Americans today would be surprised at the steepness of class stratification from the bottom of the non-upper class to the top of the upper class.

Lack of stratification recognition occurs at both the personal and aggregate levels for non-upper class people. Both difficulties in perception deny or blur stratification reality and consequently fall in line with the traditional culture. Why don't non-upper class people have this consciousness of where they personally fit in the stratification system? Partially, the lack of consciousness can be traced back to the cultural belief in individualism which stresses that each one of us in unique. Flowing from this is the rationale that we don't really belong to groups or categories of people; group membership doesn't contribute to our identities. Therefore, membership in a stratification group is not readily conceptualized. When non-upper class people do overcome these tendencies and begin to see stratified groups, they are still subject to misconceptions. Lenski (1966:87), for example, notes the tendency to exaggerate personal stratification position by inflating it.

Perception of the whole stratification system at the aggregate level by the non-upper class is even worse. We have already noted the exaggeration that America as a whole is an affluent "middle class" society. This parallels the exaggeration made at the personal level. Another problem uncovered in much stratification research is that people's understanding of the stratification system gets even foggier and more skewed as they try to perceive parts of the system removed from their own personal position. Part of the reason for this may be due to the fact that, as Parkin (1971:61) suggests, people have a tendency day in and day out to compare themselves with those who are very close to them in stratification position. People less frequently compare themselves with those who are markedly better off or worse off. When the latter comparisons are made, it is understandable that even more miscalculations are made. This suggests, once again, that non-upper class people's understanding of the whole stratification system is not even as good as their admittedly poor perception of their personal locations. Such inaccurate perceptions form a continuity with the traditional culture which encourages false assessments of the stratification system.

A marked exception to the lack of stratification awareness in America is the case of the upper class which, as Domhoff (1970) and others have demonstrated, does have class consciousness. In fact, there is evidence from Coles's (1977) research showing that upper-class children are not only conscious of their position, but also have guilt feelings over their advantages in relation to the rest of the stratification system. Interestingly, non-upper class teachers, among others, play a role in teaching such children eventually to be comfortable with their situation. The result is that the upper class, by and large, is conscious of and quite content with its position. Furthermore, the upper class consciously stands together in interesting contrast to the non-upper class.

Social Mobility

Perhaps the most glaring example of a contradiction between the American value system and the reality of stratification is in the area of social mobiltiy. As discussed above, the culture is very much centered around the belief that an individual, by means of competition and hard work, can experience a dramatic leap from rags to riches—the dream of upward social mobility. As much research has indicated, the percentage of people who experience significant mobility is very small indeed. Tully, Jackson, and Curtis (1970), for example, show that there has been a fair amount of mobility in the United States. Somewhat more has been upward rather than downward. The overwhelming majority of this mobility, however, has been within and between the white-collar and blue-collar worlds. Small leaps in mobility are made by some. Large leaps are made by very few. The latter fact is illustrated by the finding of Blau and Duncan (1967) that very few sons of blue-collar laborers rise into the professional elite during their own occupational careers.

The mobility that has been documented in America—small changes in stratification position—is not the rags-to-riches kind fantasized by those in search of the American dream. Most of the mobility, changes within and between the white- and blue-collar worlds, represents status changes within the non-upper class, but not real mobility in the system of class stratification as we have described it. This means that there is virtually no mobility from what we have described as the non-upper class into the upper class. In other words, the mobility that occurs in America seldom involves people moving from a position of not owning the means of production into a position of owning a significant share of the means of production. David Rockefeller provides an illustration. As Hoffman reports: "The American Way has been good for David, and he likes to say that free enterprise can make life good for everyone, yet in candid moments he has admitted that no person today could accumulate what he (David) was given" (Hoffman, 1971:127).

Why is it so hard to make big jumps in social mobility? The basic answer to this question is that the avenues of mobility into the upper class are severely restricted. The business world gives a good example. As mentioned previously, the small business man, "the little guy" who wants to start his own business, runs into an almost insurmountable problem. He will have to compete against much larger corporations that often already monopolize the field. We would think it funny if someone decided to start his own telephone company from scratch and compete with AT & T, but this essentially is what is done every day. The results are consistent. One half of new businesses go bankrupt during the first two years. Many of the rest barely survive.

Another version of the rags-to-riches mobility dream consists of climbing into the elite of top professionals and managers. Actually, many of these people are not upper-class but, rather, at the top of the non-upper class. Nevertheless, the limited access to such a dream is seen when one examines the cost of the basic entry requirements needed: a college education and, perhaps, a professional degree beyond the college diploma. For example, it is fairly obvious that a substantial amount of money is needed in one's family background if one wants to go to college. Resident students at some colleges today pay $10,000 per year for their expenses. This is about one half of the yearly income for the average American family. The situation is so serious that Harvard University has had to start a financial aid program for "upper-middle class" students—in other words, from the top of the non-upper class—at the undergraduate level. At the graduate level of education, as one might expect, the class bias continues. Lyons (1978), for example, reports that offers as high as $250,000 have been made to some medical schools in order to gain admission. All of this merely serves to highlight the extent to which one's inital stratification background places limits upon how far one can go in the educational system. Ultimately, with rare exception, the educational institution perpetuates the existing stratificaton system by limiting entrance into the elite of top professionals and managers.

A final point about the reality of social mobility in America needs to be made. The inability of most to experience mobility into the upper class has a feedback effect upon the cultural system in that it reinforces the emphasis upon status discussed earlier. As Reissman argues:

> With access to the upper reaches of the structure made more diffi-

cult, the person turns to a closer inspection of the position that he holds and tends to enhance it with essentially irrational and non-functional criteria that make it seem more prestigeful. Style, taste, family lineage, and occupation, for example, come to be depended upon as status criteria, while the harder features such as wealth and power, which are characteristic of relatively few of the topmost positions, come to be underplayed (1959:29).

Welfare and Wealthfare

If one is to speak accurately of the reality of the stratification in America, one must examine the systems of subsidies for the poor and the rich, known respectively as welfare and wealthfare.

The welfare system is the primary system set up to aid the bottom of the non-upper class—the poor. As noted above, the poor are pointed out by the rest of society as examples of people who have not succeeded because they are lazy and don't want to work. They also are viewed as failures who are to be blamed for their situation. Consequently, it is thought that the poor are undeserving of help; this attitude sets the groundrules for the welfare system. The poor are to be regulated (Piven and Cloward, 1971) by eligibility requirements which filter out the undeserving poor. The welfare aid levels are kept low, usually below subsistence, so that the poor are encouraged to work rather than to take a "handout." The effect of this is to create a pool of cheap labor ready to do the "dirty work" of the society for extremely low wages.

It is important to note that the negative representation of the poor which is the basis for the current welfare system is false. For example, the notion that the poor don't want to work is refuted by considerable evidence. Goodwin (1972) suggests emphatically that most of the poor do indeed want to work. They share the same desires for success and upward mobility that characterize most other non-upper class people.

"What about the unemployed poor? Why don't they work?" In response, Levitan explains that

> Despite canards about the link between laziness and poverty, most of the working-age poor who do not work are unemployed simply because they are not employable, or because jobs are not available

for them. Fully two-fifths of them are disabled. Nearly all lack educational and job skills. For the majority of these poor, some form of income support is essential to help them escape deprivation (1977:18).

Even though the poor deserve a welfare system built upon better premises, they are still blamed for the shortcomings of the one that exists. The poor still get blamed for abusing the welfare system. Actually, far from ripping off the welfare system, most poor people do not even receive benefits from programs designed to aid them. Nevertheless, the finger of blame gets pointed at those who "cheat" the welfare system. The popular, stereotyped image of the poor is the person driving to the welfare office in a Cadillac. In reality most who receive welfare still are unable to afford an adequate diet. Of course, the "chiseler" image is encouraged by the upper-class dominated media. Even the highest estimates of actual "chiseling" by welfare recipients are substantially lower than what the media leads the public to believe. An effect of this is to divide parts of the non-upper class against each other. We do not mean to excuse anyone for "cheating," but it should also be pointed out that the white-collar welfare bureaucracy is responsible for much of the welfare abuse. Finally, as we shall see, the chiseling that occurs in the welfare system is minor in comparison with the excesses of the wealthfare system.

As discussed earlier, the traditional American culture furnishes a number of rationalizations for the existence of the upper class. ("They earned their position." "They donate their money to charitable causes.") All of these arguments prop up the subsidy system for the upper class, known as wealthfare, from which the upper class does fare well.

Significant aspects of the wealthfare system include governmental purchases, governmental price supports, and export-import programs (Turner and Starnes, 1976). Such policies insure that the profits of the upper-class owned corporations are maintained at a high level. Also of tremendous importance to the wealthfare system is federal taxation at both the personal and corporate levels. As Stern (1972) suggests, this system of taxation, which includes many loopholes for the rich, is essentially "Uncle Sam's Welfare Program for the Rich." The system of loopholes described by Stern (1972) benefits the family with an annual income of one million dollars or more to the tune of $720,000—a family with an income of under $3,000 gets a "handout" of $16. The system allows many people with incomes of over $200,000 to pay *no* taxes. In 1974 there were 244 such people. The system allowed J. Paul Getty *not* to pay approximately 70 million dollars in taxes *each year*. It has enabled upper-class owned and controlled corporations such as US Steel and Ford to pay *no* taxes in some years.

Sometimes the attitude is expressed that while the upper class does benefit by the wealthfare system, it would not make much difference in terms of dollars and cents if such policies were stopped. ("There are not that many upper class people and, therefore, their 'free lunch' does not cost that much.") Such is not the case. If the system of tax loopholes were removed, it would generate 77 billion dollars according to Stern (1972). Remember also that this is but one aspect of the wealthfare system outlined above.

For purposes of comparison, it is interesting to note that the cost of a guaranteed annual income plan bringing all poor Americans out of their destitute situation has been estimated at about 30 billion dollars. This plan, however, has been labelled as a "giveaway" program too outlandish to be accepted by mainstream Americans from the white-collar and blue-collar worlds. These evaluations reflect a situation where the wealthfare system is not as visible to most people as is the welfare system, since the upper-class dominated media choose their targets for blame very carefully. These evaluations reflect a culture wherein the values tell us to blame down instead of blaming up. Finally, they create a situation where an upper-class politician can pay no taxes himself and yet base part of his political appeal to white-collar and blue-collar people on an attack of welfare chiselers.

SUMMARY AND IMPLICATIONS

The reality of stratification in America contradicts the traditional culture's view which emphasizes status stratification rather than class stratification. The very real differences in wealth and income between the top and the bottom in class stratification are not even mildly suggested by the culture. In fact, the culture encourages inaccurate appraisals of the stratification system. Furthermore, the rags-to-riches social mobility stressed by the culture is not realized in the actual lives of Americans. Mobility into the upper class is virtually non-existent. The story with respect to the welfare and wealth-fare systems is more mixed in regard to the question of whether or not there is a contradiction between the culture and the reality of stratification. Both systems implement parts of the culture that excuse the upper class and blame the poor. On the other hand, both play a role in perpetuating the existing class system by keeping the upper class rich and the bottom of the non-upper class poor. Here both systems contradict a value of great importance to the American Dream Package: equality of opportunity.

What are the implications of the above for non-upper class America demanding and achieving change in the distribution of wealth and power? The culture tends to keep people unaware of how stark class stratification actually is and how little equality of opportunity and social mobility really exist. If people do become aware, a series of rationales are offered which blame the difficulties of stratification upon the individual or the poor—but not the upper class. If the upper class is blamed, the political values of patriotism, nationalism, and democracy intercede and tend to prevent political action that challenges the existing stratification system. Also, in response to stratification problems, the culture points people in the direction of individual solutions such as upward social mobility rather than collective action such as social movements. Therefore, if successful attempts to alter the current distribution of power and wealth are to be made, a major obstacle to be dealt with is the American culture itself.

DIVISIONS AFFECTING NON-UPPER CLASS AMERICA

A major contention of this book is that the primary stratification divison in America is between the upper class and the non-
upper class. Given that the very small upper class has so much
wealth and power, a basic question keeps surfacing. Why
doesn't the very large non-upper class do something about its
position? Why doesn't the non-upper class fight for and achieve
a more equitable distribution of wealth and power? A major
reason is that the non-upper class is divided along a number of
dimensions and issues. As Domhoff suggests, the potential
for political power of the non-upper class exists because of
sheer numbers, but at the same time the non-upper class is
"hopelessly divided into income classes, religious groups,
ethnic groups, and racial groups" (Domhoff, 1967:151-152).
We amend this statement by pointing out that there are other
relevant ways in which the non-upper class is actually divided:
occupational status, attitudinal and behavioral differences,
social contact patterns, age, residential location, and sex.
All of these factors blur perception of the class system and
fracture the potential political unity of the non-upper class to
a considerable extent. Nevertheless, we do not believe that these
realities make the situation hopeless for the non-upper class.

STATUS DIFFERENCES
WITHIN NON-UPPER CLASS AMERICA

In Chapter 1 the non-upper class was described as being divided
along status lines into the white-collar world, the blue-collar

world, and the poor. At this point, we will merely indicate that finer status distinctions can be drawn which serve to make unification of the non-upper class all the more difficult.

The white-collar world has significant internal status differentiation. Its top is comprised of a variety of occupational groups which have high prestige and high incomes. Good examples of upper-level white-collar people are successful professionals such as doctors and lawyers, those in important managerial positions in the private and public sectors, and technical experts like highly skilled engineers. Perhaps as much as 10 percent of the population is located in "solid" positions of this kind. An important reason for the high prestige granted to them is that they have substantial educational credentials, usually including college and university degrees, which leads to the belief that the relatively high incomes received by the top of the white-collar world are deserved.

How high are the incomes of the top white-collar professionals? They vary from approximately $25,000 to $85,000 a year. Most of the top white-collar people, therefore, are in the position to afford comfortable suburban living. In fact, the image of affluence associated with the white-collar world exists largely because many people identify it exclusively with these upper-level white-collar positions. It is questionable, however, that even these positions lead to real affluence or influence. As we have argued before, people in this part of the white-collar world may own *some* stocks and bonds; but their ownership and control of the means of production is still small enough so that they must continue to work hard at their jobs from nine to five in order to maintain their comfortable life-style. While their stocks and bonds may cause some top white-collar workers to identify with the really affluent upper class, such thinking does not allow them to enjoy the leisure and power that is possible for the upper class. Still, the status and economic positions of the top part of the white-collar world pushes it in the direction of wanting to remain distinct from the rest of the white-collar world and the non-upper class.

At a decidedly lower level of the white-collar world are other managerial personnel and professional and technical workers of less stature. "Middle management" people and health technicians are two examples. Their status and salary levels put them on an echelon of their own in the white-collar world. At still a lower status position in the white-collar world is the vast army of sales workers and clerical workers who sell the products and do the paperwork of government and business enterprises. Almost without exception, they find themselves at the bottom of the white-collar status hierarchy. There is, however, some income variation here, especially for sales workers. A few sales workers do earn in the neighborhood of $50,000 a year. Nevertheless, this should not obscure the fact that the vast majority of sales workers earned closer to their median income of $14,000 in 1975.* Clerical workers do not have as great a salary range, and their median income of approximately $12,000 (in 1975) put them at the bottom of the white-collar world. Overall, the presence of such different levels within the white-collar world points to how it is fragmented internally. On the other hand, the economic situation of most white-collar people, whose incomes are close to the overall median income and who, therefore, have to struggle, sets them off clearly from the upper class. Another common point within the white-collar world is that many are in a position to give orders to blue-collar people. Consequently, this authority tends to separate the white-collar group from the blue-collar group.

The blue-collar world is divided in a similar fashion. At the top is a highly-skilled group of blue-collar "aristocrats," including carpenters, electricians, and plumbers. Some may earn considerably more than lower-level white-collar workers. Blue-collar craft workers, on the whole, had a median income of about $12,500 in 1975. Such skilled workers are to be distinguished from the less skilled whose income and status positions are lower. Operatives, roughly equivalent with normal factory workers had, for example, a median income of about $11,000 in 1975. At a still lower level of skill, status, and income were nonfarm laborers and service workers whose median incomes were approximately $9,000 a year. Available evidence suggests

---

*The median income data cited here for specific occupational groupings are for male workers. Women had lower incomes than did males in each of the occupational categories. The source for the data is: U.S. Bureau of the Census, 1977:411.

that the breaks in the skill hierarchy of the blue-collar world
are also correlated with the formation of distinct circles of
interaction.   Skilled   blue-collar   workers   stick   together
(LeMasters, 1975). Less skilled workers interact with each
other. The result is to harden the divisions within the blue-
collar world.

Difficulty in considering the poor as a unified group arises
because poor people have fewer social relationships than do
other segments of the stratification system. This lack suggests
that the poor are divided from one another on a personal level
even though there is a potential basis for unity in their poverty.
In other words, the poor are fragmented on an individual level.
Moreover, aggregate divisions exist among the poor. The majority of the poor, for example, work at relatively unskilled blue-
collar jobs. Others don't work at all, usually because they can't
find work due to physical and mental disabilities or to a lack
of education. This creates an obvious status hierarchy within
the world of the poor. The poor are also divided along the lines
of race, religion, nationality, age, sex, and residential location.
How, for instance, are bonds to be established between the
elderly, white, rural, poor and the young, black, city, poor?
The Bowery poor and the Appalachian poor are not only
invisible to the rest of society; to a considerable extent, they
are invisible to one another.

DIVISIONS BETWEEN NON-UPPER CLASS GROUPS

The three non-upper class groups are not only divided *within*.
A large amount of empirical research demonstrates that there
are significant attitudinal and behavorial differences *between*
the three major non-upper class stratification groups. Among
the more salient differences are those that relate to work,
religion, basic social relations, and politics. These findings
should be viewed from the perspective of their effect upon the
goal of unifying the non-upper class.

An important area of difference between the non-upper class
groups exists with respect to work experiences and attitudes.
The blue-collar/white-collar division has been described in
Chapter 1 as basically depending upon the extent to which
physical activity and mental activity are involved in one's work.

We have just finished noting how white-collar work gets more financially rewarded than blue-collar work. The experience of blue-collar work is also more immediately threatening on a day-to-day basis than is white-collar work. Levison (1974: 64-75), for example, relates a conversation among blue-collar workers at a bar where everyone is telling stories about the worst job experience they've ever heard of or actually had themselves. The conversation is friendly and humorous until one man tells about a friend of his, a young newly married man with a pregnant wife, who had his hand cut off at the wrist by factory machinery. A period of silence ensued at the bar because everyone knew personally of a work related horror story that was just as bad. Typical white-collar workers do not have anything similar in their own work experiences.

In a similar manner, attitudes of respect and disrespect towards different kinds of work show an advantage for the white-collar world. Once again, National Opinion Research Center survey results in both 1947 and 1963 indicate that white-collar workers are given considerably more prestige than blue-collar workers by the American population as a whole. This is reflected in the mass media wherein blue-collar people are often presented as worthy of derision. Archie Bunker is an example. White-collar workers such as doctors, on the other hand, are portrayed as models to be exemplified. This becomes a serious source of division between non-upper class groups because there are a substantial number of blue-collar workers who do take pride in their work and value it above the mental work of the white-collar world. In fact, many blue-collar workers (LeMasters, 1975) are suspicious of the nature of white-collar work and argue that "it's just shuffling papers." On the other side, a number of white-collar workers do not value blue-collar work. To add to the situation, many are suspicious of the blue-collar workers who have made substantial economic gains through unionization because it is thought that these gains are at the expense of white-collar people who must consequently pay high prices for goods and services.

The religious institution could bring together the blue-collar and the white-collar worlds, but it doesn't tend to do so. This can be seen in how the different non-upper class groups express their religiosity. Glock and Stark (1965:19-21) list the following among the major dimensions of religiosity: (1) intellectual—the extent of knowledge about one's religion; (2) ritual—the degree of participation in the practices of one's religion; (3) ideological—how firmly one believes in his or her religion; and (4) experiential—the degree of religious feeling or how emotionally involved in religion one becomes. Demerath (1965), among others, has shown a relationship between stratification group and how one expresses religiosity. White-collar people show higher degrees of religiosity as measured by the intellectual and ritual dimensions, whereas blue-collar people and the poor do so on the ideological and experiential dimensions.

There are a number of explanations for these findings. First, the overall higher educational attainment of white-collar workers may account for why they know more about their religion than blue-collar workers or poor people. Also, these findings lead one to conclude that those who most feel and believe their religion—blue-collar people and the poor—are the least connected to the formal religious institution in terms of practicing religious rituals such as going to church. This may actually reflect the upper-class and white-collar bias noted in many churches. This bias is demonstrated when ritual practices take on the aura of a social event where one displays status through clothes worn and cars driven to the place of worship. As a result, blue-collar people and the poor may feel uncomfortable at the ritual practices of their religion. This tendency especially appears to be the case for suburban churches. On the contrary, there are some churches in large American cities which seek to form a bridge between stratification groups by encouraging a broad mix of people to attend. In any event, these findings suggest overall that the institution of religion tends to reflect the divisions in the non-upper class rather than removing them.

Even the reality of basic social relations varies between the white-collar and blue-collar worlds. White-collar people are more likely than are blue-collar workers to become involved in voluntary organizations, groups formed for specific interests such as the American Legion or the American Civil Liberties Union (Wright and Hyman, 1958). Insofar as these organizations become vehicles for power, the result is to the political advantage of the white-collar world. On the other hand, there appears to be more social involvement on the part of blue-collar workers when it comes to family life because there is a greater tendency for these families to be extended, whereas white-collar families are more likely to be nuclear. The blue-collar family structure, therefore, provides much more contact with a variety of blood relatives outside of the immediate family (Cohen and Hodges, 1963).

There is a connection between the type of family structure and the work situation. Blue-collar people are more likely to stay with their current job if it is somewhat secure (Roach, Gross, and Gursslin, 1969:181). Seniority rules, no doubt, are operating here. White-collar workers are more likely to be geographically mobile in the pursuit of career advancement. This, for example, is encouraged by many corporations which, in fact, often link the two together for the white-collar worker. It's not uncommon for a college graduate hired by one of the major US corporations to be sent to many places throughout the country on his way up the corporate ladder. Los Angeles to Chicago to Atlanta to New York might be one partial itinerary. What we are suggesting is that the work realities of the white- and blue-collar worlds encourage different degrees of geographical mobility which, in turn, make the nuclear family more realistic for white-collar people and the extended family more possible for blue-collar people. It's difficult to keep contact with relatives if one does not live near them. Telephone advertising plays upon this: "Reach out. Reach out and touch someone . . . ."

Family life differs in other ways for the different non-upper class stratification groups. Sex roles are more traditionally stereotyped along the lines of male dominance and female submissiveness in blue-collar families than in white-collar ones (Komarovsky, 1964). White-collar families have a greater tendency to display egalitarian relationships between men and women. Likewise, the socialization of children appears to be more authoritarian in the blue-collar world. Strictness is maintained; obedience is taught. White-collar children are brought up more permissively (Vanfossen, 1979), but the goal is to produce children who will internalize the goal of success and realize it in the academic and occupational worlds.

A final area of difference between the non-upper class stratification groups is politics. We have already alluded in Chapter 2 to the differences in political power between the white and blue-collar worlds by pointing out that most congressmen at the national level come from the upper-class or the solid white-collar world. Only a handful of people have made the direct shift from a blue-collar occupation to the Congress in Washington. Aside from varying degrees of actual political power, the white-collar and blue-collar worlds are different from the standpoint of political beliefs and orientations. In general, blue-collar people are more likely to be liberal on economic issues. For example, they are more likely to be in favor of the regulation of business by the federal government or social security legislation. On the other hand, white-collar people have a greater tendency to be liberal on issues relating to civil liberties and civil rights (Stouffer, 1955).

Possibly these differences are mostly surface differences between the two groups that can be explained largely on the basis of their positions within the non-upper class. For example, it may make more sense for blue-collar people to be liberal on the economic issues cited above because they benefit more by them. Similarly, the white-collar person may be in a better position to favor civil rights for blacks because blue-collar people are more likely to be competing directly with blacks for jobs, housing, and schooling. Nevertheless, these differences, whether they are surface ones or deeper ones, serve to divide blue- and white-collar people from one another in the political arena.

SOCIAL INTERACTION WITHIN THE NON-UPPER CLASS

The divisions in the non-upper class are ultimately expressed and reinforced by the overall lack of social interaction between the white-collar and blue-collar worlds. Residential areas are quite clearly defined in terms of status group. Overall, within metropolitan America, the central city is identified with the blue-collar world and the poor. The suburban area, on the other hand, is very much dominated by the white-collar world and the upper class. The really crucial area, however, is the specific neighborhood within either the central city or the suburban town. Once one gets down to this level, it becomes even clearer that the status factor is in operation. Levison (1974), for example, points out that even when blue-collar people do live in suburbia, they live by themselves and are separated from white-collar America. Similarly, that the lower echelon of white-collar workers is willing to invest such a large proportion of their income for the privilege of residing in higher status white-collar areas (Feldman and Tilly, 1960) also attests to the desire for residential separation from the blue-collar world by white-collar people.

Residential separation highly influences the lack of contact between children from different non-upper class groups in the educational institution. Children often go to schools which are either predominantly white-collar or blue-collar. When there is a stratification mix in the schools, social separation is fostered by the development of friendship groups made up disproportionately of children from one stratification group (Hollingshead, 1949). This, in turn, merely mirrors what their parents do in their social worlds. Laumann (1966), for example, found that white-collar adults pick other white-collar people for their close friends and that a similar narrow selectivity occurs within the blue-collar world. Clubs and recreational facilities also become identified with particular non-upper class groups. Warner, for example, found that most clubs and organizations in Yankee City were identified with particular status groups. Similarly, LeMasters' (1975) study of the Oasis, a blue-collar bar, found that highly skilled blue-collar "aristocrats" were practically by themselves in frequenting the premises. Virtually no white-collar people nor poor people did so.

THE POOR AS SCAPEGOAT

Most of the comparisons that we have made pertain to the blue-collar world and to the white-collar world. In most cases, what has been said of the blue-collar world applies in some degree to the poor because when the poor work, as most do, they work in the blue-collar world—almost without exception. This would seem to suggest a potential alliance between the blue-collar world and the poor. This, however, does not tend to occur. Rather, more in evidence is the combination of the white-collar and the blue-collar against the poor. In this context, the white-collar and blue-collar worlds view the poor as separate and distinct from them. They are segregated off into city ghettos, backwood shacks, and other areas invisible to the rest of America. More generally, the poor are treated as a scapegoat.

In what ways do the poor serve as a scapegoat? A major one already discussed in Chapter 3 is that many white-collar and blue-collar people blame the poor for being where they are, at the bottom. "It's their own fault. If they had taken advantage of the opportunities available to all Americans, they wouldn't be poor," many argue. In short, the victim is blamed for his or her situation. As an elaboration of this, the poor are blamed for the consequences of poverty—bad housing, poor schooling, and a lack of food, among others. The "blaming the victim" mindset is not open to the interpretation that there are larger social and economic forces in operation which create poverty and, in turn, the consequences of poverty.

Another aspect of the poor as scapegoat story is that many blue-collar and white-collar individuals who are financially squeezed blame the poor for ripping off the welfare system. The poor, in other words, are accused of being welfare chiselers. Many non-upper class people resent that their tax dollars are being spent for this "unworthy" cause. It is true that many white-collar and blue-collar people are being squeezed by the tax system, but we contend that such anger should be directed upstairs rather than downstairs.

Why? First, the amount of chiseling by the poor is relatively negligible. Second, the welfare sytem is a control device that disciplines and regulates the poor by not providing enough financial aid for those in need. This encourages the unemployed poor to seek any kind of menial labor.* Third, the upper class

---

*As Stack (1974) indicates, the unemployed poor put pressure on employed blue-collar workers because the poor are an available source of cheap labor that can step in and take over blue-collar jobs if push comes to shove (for example, if wage demands made by blue-collar workers are perceived as too steep). This is an example of how different parts of the non-upper class get put into opposition with one another.

benefits by a wealthfare system that is more subtle, but that pays off the rich man considerably and costs the white-collar and blue-collar people substantially more than does the welfare system.

Supporting the blaming the victim mentality is the argument that the poor have a distinctive culture of poverty which causes their economic destitution. In other words, the poor have a value system that creates their poor economic situation. A central argument here is that the poor, in contrast with the rest of the non-upper class, lack the deferred gratification pattern. This essentially means that the poor aren't willing to make sacrifices now for the goal of future success. White-collar and blue-collar people are more likely to practice this pattern according to this line of thought.* As Vanfossen (1979:360) indicates, however, the actual research on this point is very cloudy and varies considerably. Some research results do not show any significant differences in the extent of deferred gratification between white-collar, blue-collar, and poor people. Other studies do demonstrate the difference hypothesized by the culture-of-poverty argument. Here, however, the question can be raised as to whether or not the differences can be explained by the different economic situations of the respective groups. It may well be that to sacrifice now eventually pays off for people from white-collar and blue-collar backgrounds, while it doesn't for the poor who must worry constantly about present survival needs such as from where the next meal is coming. Furthermore, deferred gratification may be incomprehensible to those poor who do not know of anyone from their social world who has, in fact, played out deferred gratification and been rewarded for doing so.

In a similar way, other aspects for the so-called culture of poverty—such as distinctive family and work attitudes and behavior, where they actually exist—can be understood as adaptations to the reality of poverty rather than as causes of poverty. This suggests that if efforts to change the economic

---

*It should be pointed out that there is some question about how prevalent this pattern is among white-collar and blue-collar people today. Buying by credit card and "Fly now, pay later" plans seem to emphasize immediate gratification more than is acknowledged by those who defend the culture of poverty thesis.

situation of the poor were made first, many aspects of the culture of poverty, where they actually exist, would disappear. For instance, a jobs program or a guaranteed annual-income program might well improve the economic realities of the poor so that they could think more of the future and alter any other problematic culture-of-poverty characteristics that do exist. Solutions such as the guaranteed annual income are different from those advocated by culture-of-poverty adherents who emphasize changing the values of the poor rather than their economic situation.

What finally needs to be emphasized is that culture-of-poverty arguments locate the source of blame in the poor themselves rather than in the economic system. Consequently, the arguments have been popular in America because they blame the victim. They, like other blaming strategies, also have the effect of setting one part of the non-upper class—the poor—in opposition to other segments of the non-upper class—the white-collar and blue-collar worlds. The end result is the fracturing of the non-upper class.

OTHER ALTERNATIVES TO CLASS IDENTIFICATION

Non-upper class America is also divided by a variety of other factors: age, residential location, sex, race, religion, and nationality. All of these present barriers to class identification. People can think of who they are and define themselves in terms of all of these characteristics. To the extent that personal and social identification does take place along these lines, and divisions between groups of people occur as a result, unification of the entire non-upper class becomes more difficult.

Age

Age provides an obvious example. Within non-upper class America there are age-group differences which would have to be dealt with in order for political mobilization of the non-upper class to become a reality. In particular, the omnipresent generation gap between old and young would have to be met head on. A good example of the extent to which the generation gap can divide America is the counterculture of the 1960s, which was largely, but not exclusively, championed by the young. Many older people found this value system to be totally contrary to their perception of what life is all about and how it ought to be lived. In the 1960s, old and young with the same class position probably found their age difference more salient than their class similarity. Consequently, political unification of the non-upper class was even less likely. It is interesting to note that there was less evidence of a generational difference between the old and the young in the 1970s.

Residential Location

It has already been indicated that a suburban residential location is the story for most white-collar and upper-class Americans, while in the central city is where most blue-collar and poor people make their homes. This means that there is a significant degree of homogeneity within each area. The homogeneity can blur awareness of the extent to which stratification exists within the overall society: One does not have contact with people who have drastically different stratification positions on a day-to-day basis. Contact is minimized because housing location highly influences who one interacts with—for instance, in school and leisure.

Residential location can also play a role in diverting attention away from the national class system because many people strongly identify with the region of the country that they live in such as the Northeast, the South, the Midwest, or the Far West. Conflicts often have emerged along these lines in the US. An obvious example is the Civil War between the North and the South. A modern yet milder version of such a conflict has been developing in recent years between the Sunbelt states in the South and Southwest and the rest of the country. A source of this tension is that the regions of the Northeast and the Midwest pay out about 30 billion dollars a year more than they receive back from the federal government. The obvious beneficiary is the Sunbelt. The explanation for this offerd by Kilpatrick Sale (1975) is that there has been a "power shift" to the Sunbelt. Regardless of how much of a shift in political clout has occurred, there still are strong sectional feelings. Witness the bumper sticker seen in the Sunbelt during the energy crunch of the 1970s: "Drive fast, freeze a Yankee."*

The importance of geographical location can also be analyzed from the standpoint of smaller areal units. As political commentators point out, the United States is comprised of fifty states, each with its own system of law and politics. Often the states are unresponsive to federal direction. What we can infer is that a significant number of people identify with their state of residence as much or more than they do with their national class position. (An exception to this probably is the state of New Jersey where a recent poll showed that 85 percent of its residents would rather live somewhere else.) In a number of instances, people identify strongly at an even more local level. Their identification may be with a particular town such as Westport, Connecticut, or Grosse Pointe, Michigan, or with a particular city such as Boston or San Frrancisco.

A final comment about residential location needs to be made. People change their residences quite frequently in the United States. One family in five moves every year. This geographical mobility pushes people in the direction of remaining socially separate and distinct from others because community interaction is not as important to people who are going to be moving to another area in a short period of time. Consequently, class interests shared with others are less likely to be perceived. Even when common interests are seen, geographical mobility makes it difficult for those who are mobile to become involved in collective action at the local level on the part of the non-upper class.

Sex

Sex role attitudes and behaviors of some non-upper class men and women today seem to militate against their unification for any cause. Some men, for example, are still chauvinistic and

---

*Another example of regionalism may be currently developing in the Northeast where it is becoming more generally known that the "acid rain" falling there and threatening its environment is largely caused by pollution that originates from other regions of the country. For example, 85 percent of New England's sulfate pollution comes from other regions.

have a difficult time dealing with women as equals. Also, some feminists define men as the enemy. This suggests that such men and women of the non-upper class would have a difficult time joining together for the purpose of challenging the upper class.

Sex is also relevant to the possibility of non-upper class unity in regard to development of consciousness. The 1960s and the 1970s have seen powerful movements such as those for women's liberation and gay rights develop around the sexual rights issue. While the desire for liberation is not to be challenged, questions can be raised about whether such movements aid or hurt the unification of the non-upper class. For instance, it appears that a white-collar bias has appeared in the women's liberation movement. To the extent that blue-collar and poor people feel unwelcome in the women's movement, the fractured nature of the non-upper class may be perpetuated. Furthermore, these movements have a tendency to encourage satisfaction with the stratification status quo as long as sexual rights are achieved. For example, the mainstream of the women's liberation movement stresses that a major goal for women should be to "make it" by achieving upward mobility in the occupational world. The goal of challenging the existing stratification system has taken a back seat, by and large; or it has been excluded from consideration entirely. The effect of these stances is to render a non-upper class movement unimportant because attention is shifted away from the exploitation of both women and men under existing stratification arrangements. The sexual liberation movements need an analysis that correctly identifies the source of inequality faced by both men and women: upper class ownership and control of the economy.

Ethnic Divisions

The divisions of race, religion, and nationality also play important roles in fragmenting the non-upper class.

Race Perhaps the most potent split within the non-upper class is created by the black/white division. The black population—the poor black population in particular—is singled out by white non-upper class people as the group most worthy of fear, derision, and blame. Writer Jimmy Breslin (1975) indicates this by his assessment that a major social problem in America is the fear on the part of white people that their children, their daughters in particular, will have to sit in the same classroom with Sonny Liston. The derision shown the black individual demonstrates the social anger that many white people in America have about not "making it" and being squeezed in the pocketbook.

Fear and derision find their ultimate expression in the blaming tendencies already discussed. A very important cause of such blaming is the need for mainstream white Americans to clearly identify some group underneath them. As Lewis (1978: 64-67) indicates, if no such group existed, it would further highlight the extent to which most non-upper class people have not achieved the upward mobility so central to the American Dream Package. In other words, people need to have other people who can be seen that have not achieved as much as they have. Blacks serve this role for white non-upper class Americans. According to Lewis, this is so because blacks are identified with poverty. The blaming mindset argues that blacks have "achieved" poverty or failure by laziness, for example, and thereby provide the needed framework of comparison. Individual redemption, therefore, is assured for non-upper class whites because at least they are not black.

Another slant to the significance of the black/white division is provided by Anderson (1974:293) who indicates that this racism benefits white non-upper class people in the areas of jobs, housing, and education. They have privileges over blacks that they do not want to give up. These benefits, however, are minuscule in comparison with the advantages that the upper class has over both black and white non-upper class people in terms of wealth, income, and control of the economy. Nevertheless, the latter advantages are not often perceived, while the former are. Racism, thus, fractures the non-upper class; this is in the interests of the upper class because their wealth and power might well be weakened if blacks and whites of the non-upper class ever joined together. For example, some people theorize that the real threat Martin Luther King posed for America was not in his role as a champion of black rights.

Rather, such a challenge was made when King began to direct his concern not just to blacks, but to poor people in general with an eye to forming a black/white coalition of poor people.

Religion   Religion has also served to divide the non-upper class in America quite successfully, although we are not today—twenty years after the first Catholic was elected to the presidency—as familiar with this fact as we once were. How religion can accomplish this is well illustrated by the situation in Northern Ireland. The Protestant/Catholic division historically has split the non-upper class so that the non-upper class has not perceived its common interests against the upper class as much as it otherwise might have. Breslin's (1973) novel, *World Without End, Amen*, demonstrates this pattern well. The central hero, an Irish Catholic cop from New York, goes to Northern Ireland. In the course of his visit, he discovers that the Catholics there are in a similar position to that of the blacks in America, even though both the Catholics and the Protestants are exploited by those at the top of the stratification sytem. And, the point is made clear that the unification of non-upper class Catholic and Protestant workers is very much discouraged because it is seen as a threat by the upper-class factory owners.

What about the situation in America? It is clear that the religious division of Protestant/Catholic/Jew has at times operated in a similar fashion to that in Northen Ireland. Some historians, for example, claim that there has been as much prejudice and discrimination aimed against Catholics as against any group in America. There can be no question that this partially served to prevent the non-upper class from solidifying as fully as it otherwise could have. Prejudice against the Jewish population in America has been played out in a similar manner. Antagonisms between the Protestant, the Catholic, and the Jew have at various times tended to deflect attention away from the injustices of the upper class in America. Nevertheless, it is safe to say that, while religious divisions have divided the non-upper class in the past, they do not today have as much significance as the aforementioned racial split.

Nationality   Nationality differences in the American population have also been divisive. The history of America to a large extent is one of different immigrant groups coming from Europe to America with the common hope of finding and creating a better life for themselves. Ironically, these national-ity groups have been pitted against one another in their pursuit of the American Dream Package.

One means of exploiting the nationality differences is noted by Karabel:

> Employers were quick to capitalize on the deep antipathies between workers of varying cultural and ethnic origins. One tactic was to hire workers of several different, preferably antagonistic, national-ities to work in the same plant. There management often reserved skilled positions for native-born workers or "old" immigrants, leaving for "new" immigrants only semiskilled and unskilled jobs. Ethnic division thus coincided with different skills, thereby sharpening the already existing conflicts of interest between craft workers and common laborers (1979:25-26).

Separating nationality groups by work role helped prevent the coalescence of the non-upper class. Aside from work roles, the nationality groups were also separated from one another in distinct neighborhoods which encouraged the development of social identities along the lines of ethnicity rather than stratifi-cation position. Poor Irish, poor French, and poor Italian, for example, were less likely to see and act upon their common class position than their different nationality heritages.

Overall, the large number of nationality groups in America has offered an interesting contrast with European countries which generally have had one major nationality group within their borders. One effect of nationality divisions and antagon-isms in America has been the small degree of class conscious-ness and political activity on the part of the non-upper class groups, especially when compared with their European counter-parts. For instance, while there have been strong working-class political parties in Europe, in the US they have not developed to anywhere near the same degree.

What about today? The evidence points to a decline in nation-ality cleavages over the long haul of American history. This especially seems to be the case in the white-collar suburban areas, where a certain homogenization has taken place. This supports Warner's finding that people are less likely to identify in terms of ethnicity once they rise significantly in the stratification system.

On the other hand, there has been some evidence of a revival during the 1970s in the importance placed on nationality identification by groups such as the Poles and the Italians. Partially, this can be interpreted as a response to the interest in ethnic.roots demonstrated by blacks and the increase in black power during the 1960s and 1970s. Also, this resurgence of nationality identification on the part of some groups may be a response to a failure to make significant progress in stratification mobility by following the formula of casting off the culturally identifying characteristics of nationality background. In other words, it appears that some nationality groups have nothing to lose by fostering an interest in their heritages. Of course, from this book's perspective, such a revival of interest in nationality as a source of personal and social identification could potentially fracture the non-upper class.

Overall, the ethnic divisions of race, religion, and nationality have been critical in preventing the development of class consciousness and political activity on the part of the non-upper class. As Rossides (1976:428) and others suggest, it is not possible to explain the lack of a more revolutionary working class in America unless such differences are examined closely.

OVERALL SIGNIFICANCE OF NON-UPPER CLASS DIVISIONS

This chapter has concentrated upon a variety of divisions within the non-upper class: status, age, residential location, sex, race, religion, and nationality. From each of these bases of division, distinctive subcultures tend to form. Depending upon where one fits with respect to these splits (old or young, black or white, male or female) one wears a special set of lenses through which the world is perceived. These same divisions become alternative bases of personal and social identification—alternative to class identification. Furthermore, scapegoats for frustrations can and do get formed. Consequently, not only the poor serve as a target for blame, so also do blacks and Jews, among others. Overall, the divisions affecting non-upper class America take attention away from class stratification and block the possible unity of the non-upper class. Any serious effort at politically organizing the non-upper class will have to take these divisions into account.

AMERICAN INSTITUTIONS AND STRATIFICATION

As we grow up and eventually live out our adult day-to-day lives, we are constantly in contact with society's major institutions: religion, the family, the educational system, the economy, and the political system. Each of these institutions teaches us the "rules of the game" that we are supposed to play by. One of these rules is that the stratification sytem is justified and not to be challenged. The major American institutions constantly reinforce this lesson, and consequently perpetuate the existing stratification system.

RELIGION

Through history the religious institution has served many functions for society. As Durkheim (1948) noted, religion can increase the cohesion and solidarity of society's members. Others have discussed how religion can help people deal with the ultimate difficulty of making sense out of life and death. Of more direct importance to us here is the role that religion plays in connection with stratification.

The religious institution can either prop up or challenge the existing stratification system. As is the case with most institutions, historically the tendency has been more in the direction of the former than the latter. In so doing, the religious institution accomplishes social control. Or, in traditional Marxist terms, religion serves as an opiate for the people. By stressing an other-worldly orientation, religion gives people the escape valve of a "pie in the sky." Why not accept one's current meager stratification position and not challenge the system of inequality if, in fact, the meek are going to inherit the earth?

An interesting example of how Catholicism in the United States has operated as an institution of social control is that some upper-class Protestants have actually donated large sums of money to the Catholic Church on the grounds that the church would keep their members in line against socialism or any other revolutionary alternative. Railroadman James Hill, for example, gave a million dollars to build a Catholic seminary because he believed the church to be the only institutional authority respected and feared by the new Catholic immigrants who made up a significant percentage of the working class (Baltzell, 1958:224).

Research carried out by Gary Marx (1967) tends to confirm the role attributed to religion by Karl Marx. In particular, Gary Marx's research indicates that religious involvement among blacks was related to a lack of civil rights militancy during the 1960s. Those not religiously involved showed a greater likelihood of being militant. This suggests that religion encourages people to accept social injustice rather than to fight it. One should point out, however, that religion very definitely does have the potential to lead people to questioning and challenging sources of injustice such as the stratification system. As Gary Marx argues, there is also a "Social Gospel" strand to religion. More on this later, but first more discussion of how religion serves to perpetuate stratification is in order.

Because churches need money to survive, the messages conveyed by them must not offend those church members who give financial support. In other words, there is a built-in tendency for the religious institution not to rock the stratification boat too severely. Otherwise, it too will sink. As we saw earlier in the Lynds' research, the upper class has had a large impact upon churches through their donations and financial clout.

Another tendency has been for the churches to follow the migration pattern of the white-collar world: out of the central city and into suburbia. Along with this the concern of the church has shifted away from the blue-collar world, poverty, and race. Similarly, churches tend to draw their members from neighborhoods of homogenous stratification makeup. Thus, not only does the church separate the upper class from the non-upper class, but the non-upper class status divisions are reinforced when the white-collar, blue-collar, and poverty groups have their own churches. In other words, the religious institution tends to reflect existing stratification divisions rather than remove them.

Far from criticizing the cultural system that defends and rationalizes the existing stratification system, the religious institution in America tends to reinforce it. As Will Herberg (1955) argues, the dominant American religions of Protestantism, Catholicism, and Judaism have a common core: the celebration of the American way of life. The traditional American cultural system discussed earlier is the centerpiece of all three major religions. To politically challenge the stratification system, by and large, is not supported.

The relative lack of support given to political challenge of the status quo by the religious institution is reflected in the relationship that has evolved in recent years between religious leaders and political leaders. Basically, political leaders use religious leaders as window dressing to provide a show of support and to lend credibility and a moral tone to their administrations. Thus, we have become accustomed to seeing Presidents appear on Sunday morning with a religious leader such as Billy Graham. The political leader gains by this connection because it looks good to be allied with the religious hierarchy. Other points need emphasis here. This relationship shows that religious leaders, when they are seen in America, tend not to be out in front on social issues. Rather, they are pulled in to give credibility to a political leader and his or her programs. And, the religious leader selected for display must be in general ideological agreement with the political leader. Thus, a Nixon chooses to be seen with a Norman Vincent Peale rather than a Daniel Berrigan.

Religion as an institution in America, for the most part, has served the interests of social control, and it has usually dragged its feet on social justice issues. But, as Gary Marx indicated, it does not have to be this way since Social Gospel messages abound in the major religions. This strand runs through the prophetic books of the Old Testament, the Gospel of St. Matthew in the New Testament, and some of the papal encyclicals. (Populorum Progressio of Pope Paul VI is an example.) The Social Gospel messages against social inequality have obviously been taken to heart by people such as Martin Luther King. And, today, groups move against social inequality that find similar support from the religious institution. The question left unanswered, however, is how to bring this spirit into the center of mainstream American religion.

THE FAMILY

A pivotal institution for the reproduction of social inequality in America is the family. It does this in a number of ways. First, the family prepares people for the acceptance of the social stratification system in general and their particular places in it. Second, when people perceive a need to challenge the stratification system, the pressures of day-to-day family life make it difficult to do so.

How does the American family engender an acceptance of the stratification system? As we grow up in families, we become familiarized with the concept of hierarchy. This notion of some people, usually adults, giving orders and others, usually children, executing them becomes ingrained in us as we witness countless situations of social interaction. This is true even though, as Slater (1977:48-67) argues, the American family compared with other family systems is relatively democratic. The net effect of these experiences is that we learn to accept heirarchy not only in family situations but also in the churches, schools, workplaces, political arenas, and in the overall stratification system.

Particular characteristics of the traditional American family system also play a role in preparing us. Of all the possible family systems, the small nuclear family system is the one most likely to emphasize competition rather than cooperation. Extended families, by blood or by choice, tend to reverse this priority. Consequently, children growing up in nuclear families learn the competitive rules of the game that prevail in the educational and economic institutions.

Another structural characteristic of the American family system that pushes in the same direction is the full-time mother role played by a still significant percentage of women. As Slater

(1976:70-73) indicates, the typical excess concern with the mother role on the part of American women diminishes the sources of fulfillment for them. They may not have sought employment outside of the home as much as they could have; consequently, they have to fulfill most of their needs vicariously through their children. The effect of this on the children, according to Slater, is that they tend to become vain and very competitive. As a result, they fit into the existing educational and economic systems quite nicely. The family system has done its job well.

So far we have discussed the family's preparation of people for the stratification system on a fairly general level. The family teaches us to accept hierarchy and to be competitive. But the family system also helps to reproduce the existing division of labor by preparing people for a specific range of occupations similar to the ones held by their parents. As Kohn (1969) has observed, self-direction is more characteristic of parents with higher status jobs, whereas conformity to external authority is apparent for those with lower status jobs. These patterns are conditioned by one's work experience and are transmitted to one's children through family socialization. When the children go to work themselves, they are predisposed towards occupations similar to those of their parents.

Also, family life produces many pressures which deter people from challenging the stratification system. What are some of these pressures? For one thing, in the face of a confusing world, the family is still perceived as a refuge from the drudgery experienced at school or work, and from the political chaos of the world. As such, the family must soothe a lot of sores and pains. Unfortunately, emotional comfort, as well as other family functions, must be carried out for most Americans by a small nuclear family. If we think of each adult member of the family as an emotional shock absorber for the other adult members, we are struck by the fact that adults in most nuclear families have only one other adult to rely upon for emotional support and comfort. We have one emotional shock absorber who is responsible for touching and understanding all the facets of our multidimensional personalities. Often this pressure is coupled with the desire for a permanent continuation of romantic love with that one other adult. The net effect of these demands is that most families experience a considerable amount of stress. Clear evidence of this is that the divorce rate currently is fifty percent. One out of two marriages ends in divorce. Research also shows much dissatisfaction within surviving marriages. Even happy marriage partners report that conflict is a major form of interaction for them.

All of the evidence suggests that American people must invest a lot of energy in an emotional endeavor that is time-consuming, frustrating, and very often ultimately disappointing. People have a difficult time making family situations work successfully. To suggest changing the stratification system seems far removed from many people's day-to-day realities and capabilities when they are often in the midst of family struggles. If individuals spend nine to five everyday working and evenings attempting to make family life sustaining, there's little time left for anything else. Even if problems relating to the concentration of wealth and power are perceived, many people simply have no time left over for the political activity required to challenge the current system of inequality.

Not only is political activity on a large scale rendered difficult, but the family situation also militates against questioning and challenging the rules of the game in the economic institution. To tell off the boss in the workplace, for example, threatens the family finances. How often do we hear people express that if it were not for family ties, they would change their work situations?

There are, of course, significant changes going on which may affect how the American family system now props up the overall system of inequality. Extended families by choice, where groups of people consisting of families and single adults voluntarily decide to live out day-to-day family life together, are one such option. The rural and urban communes of the 1960s and 1970s are examples. Such "families" involve a greater number of people in carrying out the functions of the family and thereby relieve some of the pressures currently felt by the nuclear family system. Communal family units are also much more egalitarian and less hierarchical. Furthermore, according to Slater (1976:156-157), they are also much more likely to produce children who value cooperation over competition and who are less prone to narcissistic individuality. Consequently, the reproduction of the existing stratification system is undermined by these families.

Commual groups also can and often do challenge the current stratification system by becoming more self-sufficient in producing their own food and shelter. This cuts into upper-class profits and is, therefore, an important component of overall opposition to the current system of inequality in America. But, and we see this as important, the communal movement cannot be the only component. The communal movement can be allowed to exist by the upper class as long as a critical mass does not turn to it. Other sources of opposition need to be fostered and developed.

Another change in the family institution is the women's liberation movement. This has a positive effect in that the full-time mother role is discouraged. The movement encourages women to develop more avenues for fulfillment. As a result, children are freed from a pattern that currently relates to their development into vain and overly competitive people. This then ultimately threatens the stratification system. A side note: the women's liberation movement should be cautious about falling into the trap of just encouraging women to "move up" the occupational ladder. This movement has the opportunity to emphasize cooperation and sharing instead of competition and thereby challenge the existing stratification system on a broad scale.

EDUCATION

There is a rich tradition of social science research that demonstrates how the educational institution, by and large, reproduces the existing stratification system from one generation to the next. This reproduction can be seen through all levels of the educational system: grammar school, high school, and college.

The pioneering community studies of the Lynds, Warner, and Hollingshead discussed in Chapter 1 all showed how education perpetuates the stratification system. The Lynds found that the public school board was heavily influenced by the business class, as was the local state teachers' college. Warner also found that school boards were dominated by people from the top of the stratification system whose children, in turn, were the beneficiaries of favoritism on the part of teachers in grades received and honors bestowed.

Hollingshead, in his research, found similar biases on the part of the public school system. The tracking system, for example, put children from the upper stratification groups on the College Prep route almost routinely—and exclusively; a similar bias existed in the granting of academic awards. All of this information served to confirm Hollingshead's hypothesis that the social behavior of adolescents in Elmtown "appears to be related functionally to the positions their families occupy in the social structure of the community" (Hollingshead, 1949:9). A large array of data also showed how children from lower stratification positions suffered discrimination from their fellow students of higher stratification position by being excluded from cliques, gangs, and dating relationships. The overall effect of the discrimination by the school system and the students was that the existing stratification system was reaffirmed and made legitimate. Instead of operating as a place of equal opportunity and as an avenue for social mobility, as many Elmtowners believed it did, the public school was found to perpetuate the status system from generation to generation. The public school enforced stratification.

The trends observed in earlier research have also been demonstrated by more current research. Perhaps one of the most telltale bodies of research deals with the expectations that teachers have of various students' abilities to learn (their educability). Rosenthal and Jacobson (1968) found that the self-fulfilling prophecy operates. If teachers think that certain students are talented, these students will perform well. If teachers have low expectations of students these become translated into poor performance. Of central importance to us is the question of whether or not the class background of children affects what teachers expect. The answer is yes (Rist, 1970). Teachers expect children from the bottom of the stratification system not to do well and children from the top of the stratification system to succeed. And, of course, these expectations are fulfilled. This is one of the ways in which the class structure gets reproduced by the educational institution.

Neighborhood public schools help reproduce the class structure to some extent. The local property tax substantially determines the financial support of the public educational system. The tax, in turn, is highly influenced by the class background of the neighborhood. As a result, central city schools and their students suffer, while suburban schools and their students benefit.

Evidence also suggests that tracking within schools is another mechanism of reproduction. As Aronowitz notes, "Students placed in lower tracks within the grades learn early in their school careers that these tracks represent their failure. Even if they succeed in terms of the 'subject matter,' the labels assigned to lower tracks restrict their horizon of future occupations" (Aronowitz, 1973:75). Does class background affect tracking? In her review of the relevant literature, Vanfossen (1979:262) suggests that the answer once again is yes.

The phenomenon of tracking suggests that the educational institution is a placement bureau for the occupational structure. (As a Bob Dylan song advises, "Twenty years of schooling and they put you on the day shift.") Schools essentially develop people who will man the various occupational positions in the economic structure. How are people prepared for particular hierarchical levels within the division of labor? Bowles and Gintis respond by saying that

> Different levels of education feed workers into different levels within the occupational structure and, correspondingly, tend toward an internal organization comparable to levels in the hierarchical division of labor. As we have seen, the lowest levels in the hierarchy of the enterprise emphasize rule-following; middle levels, dependability, and the capacity to operate without direct and continuous supervision; while the higher levels stress the internalization of the norms of the enterprise. Similary, in education, lower levels (junior and senior high school) tend to severely limit and channel the activities of students. Somewhat higher up the educational ladder, teacher and community colleges allow for more independent activity and less overall supervision. At the top, the elite four-year colleges emphasize social relationships conformable with the higher levels in the production hierarchy (1976:132).

The kind of schooling received by a student prepares him or her for a specified range of positions within the job market according to Bowles and Gintis. And, as discussed earlier, initial class position highly influences educational opportunities. The net effect is that the educational institution reproduces the class structure. Class background determines one's education which, in turn, prepares one for an occupational future roughly comparable to that of one's parents.

Is it really all that simple? Critics of Bowles and Gintis such as Ravitch (1978) have taken them to task for not giving enough attention to the fact that the public school system historically has given lowly-stationed immigrants the where-withal to rise out of poverty and into "affluent" America. Nevertheless, Ravitch admits that one's family's class back-ground does have an influence upon educational attainment and occupational success. However, she tends to minimize its role. Also, Ravitch exaggerates the actual amount of mobility experienced by Americans through schools. For example, she enthusiastically cites Blau and Duncan's (1967) finding that almost ten percent of the sons of manual workers rose into the elite occupations such as the professions. On the other hand, what happened to the other ninety percent? In truth, most mobility in America has not been that dramatic. It has amounted primarily to a minor reshuffling of people within the non-upper class. There has been very little mobility from the non-upper class into the upper class. The issue of the interpreta-tion of data is obviously at hand here, but we agree more with Bowles and Gintis than Ravitch. The educational institution certainly has allowed for some individual mobility, but it has more widely served to reproduce the class structure. Let's continue our examination of this more closely by looking at information showing the connection between class background and college education.

How is college attendance affected? According to the US Census (1974:43-44) in 1973, 53.7 percent of the college-aged population from families with an annual income of $15,000 or more attended college, whereas only 12.7 percent of the college-aged from families with an annual income of under $3,000 were at school. Clearly, class background influences attendance—just as it does who graduates. Sewell and Shah (1967:10) report data indicating that 42 percent of offspring from the highest socioeconomic status graduate, compared with only 7.5 percent of those from the lowest socio-economic status.

The story does not end here, however. There is a definite stratification within colleges and universities. Generally, the higher one's stratification position, the greater the chance of going to the "best" schools, which, in turn, leads to the "best" jobs. At the bottom is the two-year community college which Karabel (1972) argues serves as a negative track for non-upper class offspring of blue-collar parents. The high dropout rate at such schools is indicative of the frustration of students who desire upward mobility. A middle tier, above the community-college level, consists of four-year public colleges and universities. A higher percentage of white-collar students attends these schools, but very few upper-class students do so. An exception to this occurs in the case of some of the well-known public universities in the western states, such as the University of California at Berkeley, where a somewhat large number of upper-class students attend. At the top of the stratification system of colleges and universities are the elite private colleges and universities such as Harvard, Yale, and Princeton. Here a high percentage of upper-class youth goes to school. This does not mean that a substantial number of non-upper class people do not go to such schools. In recent years there have been a number of scholarships set aside for the sons and daughters of the non-upper class. This serves to "cream off" talent from the top of the non-upper class and to rationalize the overall system of inequality. Also, it is important to note that there is stratification within a particular elite college or university. This occurs through club memberships which tend to segregate upper-class students from the rest of the student population. Exclusive clubs such as the Porcellian Club at Harvard, the Ivy Club at Princeton, and the Fence Club at Yale have served this function.

All of the information presented so far implies that the educational institution in America selects people out by class background and prepares them for the same class position in their occupational lives. Consequently, the stratification status quo is reproduced. Aside from being a placement bureau, however, there are other ways in which the educational institution perpetuates the stratification system. Possibly less obvious to the observer of higher education is that the research funding for many universities and their academic personnel is closely connected with government agencies, among them, the Department of Defense. While sometimes this situation is benign, in other cases the resulting reearch transforms the educational institution into a servant of the upper class. On the other hand, during the Viet Nam War, some of these same universities produced articulate spokesmen against the military-industrial complex. There is a similar ambivalence in regard to how the universities treat the poor. Well publicized are the academic and financial programs of the 1960s and 1970s designed to aid students with a background of poverty. Less well publicized is the fact that private urban universities enjoy a tax-free status that ultimately is a disservice to urban populations, which are disproportionately made up of blue-collar and poor people. Moreover, some institutions, such as Harvard and Columbia, have had substantial financial interests in the substandard housing near to them. In effect, they are slum landlords.

A host of educational reforms have been suggested to correct educational inequities: compensatory education, busing, the pooling of local property tax revenues for education, and open education. Such plans, if properly articulated, could serve the purpose of establishing more equal educational opportunity for all. (An interesting note here is that so far open education has been made more available to students from the top half of the stratification system than it has been to students from the bottom half. Some suggest that this is related to the goal of reproducing the existing division of labor because children from the top half of the stratification system will be filling the more "creative" decision-making functions.) In any event, the evidence offered by Jencks (1972) is that even if educational equality is achieved, it won't by itself bring economic equality. Jencks and others suggest that ultimately the key changes in America will have to take place in the economic and political spheres.

WORK

The experiences of the average American in the religious, family, and educational institutions condition her or him for the stratification that exists within the economic institution. This economic stratification has already been explored at some length in Chapter 2 when we contrasted the income, wealth, and taxation situations of the upper class and the non-upper class. Behind the large differences between these two groups, one finds that the upper class owns and controls the means of production while the non-upper class does not. What this, in turn, leads to is markedly different work situations for the two classes. The upper class does not have to work, although many of its members do work in order to acquire further power and prestige; the non-upper class instead does have to work for survival. The world of work, which is an economic necessity for the non-upper class, reinforces the existing stratification system and becomes a major obstacle in the path of change.

The structure of work in the American economy obscures the reality of the class system by promising economic security and psychological fulfillment. In this vein, some social science research has suggested that even blue-collar workers have become affluent and enjoy the "good life." To a considerable extent the people observed by LeMasters (1975) conform to this portrait, but it is important to note that his sample consisted of "blue-collar aristocrats" who worked in a variety of construction trades. The picture developed by Levison (1974:90-95) of the blue-collar world covers the entire spectrum of such occupations and offers a sharp contrast to LeMasters's research. Levison indicates that, aside from having meager incomes, most blue-collar workers have poor fringe benefits when it comes to pension plans (one half have no private pension plan), vacations (one half get two paid vacation weeks after working for two years), and sick leave (only one in five get full pay when ill). All of this hardly spells affluence.

In response to the affluent worker notion, bear in mind the basic fact that most blue-collar and white-collar families have incomes very close to or below the amount that the Bureau of Labor Statistics estimates it costs to survive in very modest style. Remember, these families are expected to keep their toasters for thirty-three years. In terms of wealth, the vast majority of white-collar and blue-collar workers own very little or nothing at all. Furthermore, the facts about social mobility do not foreshadow things getting better in the future.

What about psychological fulfillment? In point of fact, most workers in America feel alienated and powerless in their jobs. Day-to-day survival becomes a realistic goal for many. As Studs Terkel says, "To survive the day is triumph enough for the walking wounded among the great many of us" (Terkel, 1972: XI). This situation is reflected in a major government report, *Work in America,* which indicates that two out of every five white-collar workers and one out of every four blue-collar workers are satisfied with their jobs. Many are decidedly unsatisfied with their work. Aronowitz quotes a factory worker: "I never think about my job. In fact, I try to do everything I can to forget it. If I concentrated on thinking about it, I'd go crazy" (Aronowitz, 1973:26).

The man who made the above statement is a person whose job involves doing the same task over and over again—putting two clips on a hose. This contrasts with nineteenth-century capitalism, a system under which workers, according to Breecher (1979), actually had control of the productive process and had a "craft" role. As Braverman (1974) notes, modern trends of scientific management have robbed workers of this source of fulfillment by breaking work down into small, repetitive steps. Each worker on the assembly line does a few steps repeatedly at a fast pace. Not only is each worker an appendage of the machine; each worker is treated as a machine. Modern capitalism has introduced a process that turns men and women into robots, stripping them of the need to be creative in the work process. As a result, boredom and tedium are basic aspects of work. Could anything be more alienating?

What happens for the blue-collar worker on the assembly line also happens for white-collar people working in the bureaucracy that characterizes business and government. C. Wright Mills (1951) was one of the first to point out the increasing proletarianization of the white-collar worker. He noted how white-collar work was becoming more routinized, mechanized, and stripped of skill. In fact, outside of the heavy labor required in some blue-collar work, Mills saw an increasing similarity between white-collar and blue-collar work. Braverman (1974) continues this theme by pointing out how it is only a relatively few white-collar workers who actually carry out the mental tasks of thought and planning. On the other hand, many white-collar workers—clerical workers for example—have work that actually emphasizes manual over mental labor.

A further similarity between the work conditions of white-collar and blue-collar workers is that they are subordinate to others in the work situation and consequently must be submissive. We accept this as true for the person on the assembly line; but it is also true for the white-collar worker. Joseph Heller (1974) describes well the bureacratic situation of many white-collar workers in his novel *Something Happened* when he depicts a typical business office. Each of the workers is afraid of those who run the company. Furthermore, each of the workers is encouraged to be afraid of every other worker. Domination and submission result for most. The central character of the book, Bob Slocum, realizes the inability of the average individual to challenge the system. He wonders to himself about what would happen if he rebelled. His answer is that nothing would happen. Any act of disobedience or defiance would have no effect. In fact, Heller suggests that bureaucracies take on a life of their own, independent of the people working for them. "As far as the company is concerned, no one needs anyone. It goes on by itself. It doesn't need us. We need it" (Heller, 1974:419). The general drift of the bureaucracy's independent life is automatically to support the status quo, and this has obvious ramifications for the persistence of inequality. Bold steps are squelched. Attempts at change run directly into the wall created by the red tape of bureaucracies.

The system of inequality is also maintained by a number of divisions within the workplace. Even though the white-collar and blue-collar worlds are much closer in actual working conditions than is commonly thought, the status differences between them persist. The consistency of the National Opinion Research Center's occupational prestige ratings over time indicates this. White-collar work gets more status and respect than does blue-collar work. One can see the lack of respect for blue-collar work in part of a conversation between Tally of *Tally's Corner* and the book's author, Elliot Liebow:

> Liebow: "Nobody knows everything. One man is a doctor so he talks about surgery. Another man is a teacher, so he talks about books. But doctors and teachers don't know anything about concrete. You're a cement finisher and that's your specialty."
>
> Tally:　"Maybe so, but when was the last time you saw anybody standing around talking about concrete?" (1967:62).

The theme of no respect is also clearly seen in the research of Sennett and Cobb (1973). The study showed that the thing most sought by the blue-collar workers was respect. This concern, in fact, was so all-consuming that it was more important than a direct challenge of the stratification system which they knew to be the cause of many of their problems. In fact, gaining respect appeared to be a necessary precondition before any challenge could ever be mounted.

The white-collar/blue-collar split is not the only workforce division that serves to divide the non-upper class. Breecher (1979), for example, cites the role of job ladders and hierarchies in preventing the development of a homogeneous workforce which might unite. Forms of payment, such as piece rate, have been devised to make workers compete with one another. Also, historically, hiring has been done with the goal of dividing workers. "It was common practice for industrial employers to hire from a wide range of ethnic groups in order to have a divided labor force that would have difficulty organizing" (Breecher, 1979:11). Furthermore, what was attempted was an allocation of particular kinds of work to specific ethnic groups with an eye toward maximizing the animosity between workers. This was accomplished, for example, when old immigrants were assigned to skilled labor positions and more recent immigrants were only allowed to work in less skilled jobs. The superimposition of stratified work roles upon the already existing ethnic differentiation, for the most part, proved to be very effective in preventing the unification of the non-upper class workforce. Interestingly, the provocative 1978 movie *Blue Collar* shows how the aim of dividing the workforce is still held in the American workplace. The movie shows how the splits of black worker/white worker and the old worker/young worker are manipulated in order to keep people working while they direct their frustrations at one another rather than against the owners of the workplace.

Perhaps the sharpest division within the non-upper class workforce—and the most difficult to overcome—is between the poor and the rest of the non-upper class. The poor are a labor pool that provides status and economic benefits for the rest of America. As indicated elsewhere, the poor serve the function of making the rest of the population feel good about themselves. At least, the rest aren't at the bottom. Also, the poor provide the population with a cheap labor supply to do the dirty work of the society.

Significantly, because the poor are separated from the rest of the non-upper class, the potential for unification of the entire non-upper class is not realized. An example of this is that organized labor has for the most part steered clear of attempting to unionize the poor who are in unskilled occupations. When this is coupled with the historic tendency of the white-collar world to exhibit disdain at the thought of unionizing, the failure of the labor movement to unite and represent the entire non-upper class becomes all the more apparent. Instead, we see that Big Labor concerns itself almost exclusively with the skilled blue-collar worker. Also, as Domhoff (1970) and others have suggested, Big Labor sometimes has been co-opted by those in control of the larger economic system. When this has been the case, Big Labor has presented no serious threat to the capitalist system.

What are the consequences of the issues relating to the structure of work? They are simple and straightforward. First, division within the workforce keep hostilities concentrated within rather than focused upon the oppression caused by the upper class. Second, the alienating nature of work robs people's lives of meaning. This can be seen clearly in the boring and tedious work of both the blue-collar assembly line and the white-collar bureaucracy. People's mental and physical energies are sapped by their work as they seek day-to-day survival. When these stresses are compounded by the demands of daily family living, it is easy to see that most people have little or no energy left over for getting involved in any activity, much less political activity aimed at the upper class. Third, the hierarchical structure of work wherein a few managers dominate and the great mass of workers take orders has deleterious effects upon the possibility of social change. If people have to accept inequality in the workplace, how can we expect them to challenge the broader stratification system which, in truth, is determined by people's places in the process of economic production? Also, if people have to take orders at work, how can we expect them to act democratically in the political institution? These questions suggest negative answers which this book does not agree with, as will be seen in the next chapter.

One additional comment on work in America: Possible solutions to the inequalities of the workplace are discussed and sometimes implemented, but they should be carefully scrutinized. Consider Braverman's negative evaluation of various worker participation plans:

> They represent a style of management rather than a genuine change in the position of the worker. They are characterized by a studied pretense of worker "participation," a gracious liberality in allowing the worker to adjust a machine, replace a light bulb, move from one fractional job to another, and to have the illusion of making decisions by choosing among fixed and limited alternatives designed by a management which deliberately leaves insignificant matters open to choice. One can best compare this style of management with the marketing strategy followed by those who, having discovered that housewives resent prepared baking mixes and feel guilty about using them, arrange for the removal of the powdered egg and restore to the consumer the thrill of breaking a fresh egg into the mix, thereby creating an "image" of skilled baking, wholesome products, etc. (1974:39).

Braverman implies that genuine worker participation should involve a real input into the total decision-making process. This ultimately means sharing in decisions about what things are to be produced, how they are to be produced, and how they are to be distributed throughout society.

POLITICS

Efforts to deal with the class inequities of the economic institution ultimately have to deal with the political institution and its governmental structures at the federal, state, and local levels. To understand the political institutions, one must understand the distribution of power in the population. By power we mean the ability to influence decisions that affect one's life. As seen in Chapter 2, the upper class is essentially a ruling class at the national level.

Research indicates that what holds true at the national level also occurs at the local level. The classic piece of empirical research illustrating this argument is the study of the power structure carried out by Hunter (1953) in Atlanta, Georgia. In a city of roughly 500,000 people, it was found that only about 40 men, mostly from the business world, were responsible for the really important decisions affecting the future of the community. In other words, the power elite thesis was proven at this more local level. Studies of power at less than the national level do not always confirm such a concentration of power. Dahl's (1961) study of New Haven, for example, is a classic exception. On the other hand, the majority of studies do exhibit this concentration according to Walton (1966).

The concentration of power in the hands of the upper class makes it the ruling class. As mentioned in Chapter 2, the work of Mills and Domhoff demonstrated this. Upper-class power was wielded through political campaign funding, the flow of personnel back and forth between government and big business, the nature of governmental regulatory agencies, and the government subsidization of the upper class and its big businesses. Also noted were difficulties with alternative conceptions of the distribution of power in America such as the pluralist argument and the power of the vote argument.

We will not reiterate all of the specific points made in Chapter 2 but merely note a few basic ones. First, the upper class is a ruling class. Second, the non-upper class has the potential to exert its influence due to its sheer numbers. This influence could be used to alter considerably the current distribution of wealth and power.

There are many obstacles which have to be overcome if the potential of the non-upper class is to be realized. First, there is a lack of solidarity within the non-upper class. There are many splits and divisions in the non-upper class, discussed in Chapter 4, which have to be dealt with if the requisite solidarity is to be achieved.

A second major obstacle is the fact that may non-upper class Americans "buy" a value system that leads them to believe in and defend the existing stratification system. Key here are: 1) the American Dream Package; 2) blaming patterns that are directed against the individual person and the poor rather than the upper class; 3) political values of nationalism, patriotism, and democracy; and 4) the emphasis upon status rather than class discussed in Chpater 3. A question, of course, must be asked as to why the non-upper class buys these cultural patterns if they are in fact detrimental to their sociological health. And, part of the answer lies in that it is in the interest of the upper class to see these patterns "bought." Consequently, the upper class uses its influence to see that this happens not only in the economy and the political order, but also in the religious, family, and educational institutions. Upper-class influence on the media also needs to be considered seriously. One gets a chill, for example, when one hears the Bell Telephone ad that states: "The System is the Solution." Not only do we have no alternative but to buy a phone from AT & T, the ad also tells us that we have no political alternative but the current system.

Another major obstacle to non-upper class political action is the prevailing attitude of "you can't fight city hall." There are many things that feed into this attitude. First, a non-upper class that exhibits little solidarity can not raise the money needed for the political clout to fight back. Also, if you have to take order at work, it is a big shift to participate in an active way in the political process. Furthermore, non-upper class people caught in the 9 A.M.-5 P.M./5 P.M.-9 A.M. survival scenario find it difficult to summon the energy needed for political involvement. What all of this results in is a high level of apathy. We already cited the fact that only 50 percent of the voters bother to vote in presidential elections. In the same vein, a 1974 CBS poll revealed that only 14 percent of the electorate could name who was running for the national congressional office in their congressional district. Surely such lack of political knowledge has to be traced back to apathy. The apathy, in turn, may be viewed as a realistic response to upper-class control of the political process. If both major political parties are controlled by the upper class, does it matter if you vote for candidate X or candidate Y?

The obstacles of a lack of non-upper class solidarity, a culture that defends the existing stratification system, and political apathy all will have to be considered seriously by those who want positive political and economic changes in the situation of the non-upper class. One means of attempting to create such changes is for large numbers of the non-upper class to organize a social movement aimed at fighting the concentration of wealth and power in upper-class hands. We turn to this possibility in Chapter 6.

REACTIONS TO THE CONCENTRATION OF
INCOME, WEALTH, AND POWER

The concentration of wealth and power in upper-class hands proves that substantial inequality marks American society. The dominant American cultural system rationalizes this inequality. A variety of divisions and differences between and within non-upper class stratification groups makes it difficult for non-upper class America to unify in order to demand and achieve change in the distribution of wealth and power. Furthermore, various institutional settings with which we have contact on a day-to-day basis inculcate and defend inequality. We must evaluate the extent to which non-upper class America actually has challenged the status quo of inequality in the recent past and how likely it is to do so in the near future. What political options for dealing with the concentration of power and wealth have been or could be exercised by the non-upper class?

SOCIAL MOVEMENTS OF THE 1960s AND 1970s

The non-upper class could form a broadly based social movement that challenges the concentration of wealth and power. A social movement exists when a large number of people unite and act together for the purpose of either making or resisting change in one or more societal situations. There are a variety of different kinds of social movements. For our purposes, we will concentrate on just three of them. A **resistance movement** exists when its driving motive is to return to an earlier social arrangement. Its prevailing sentiment is that social change has progressed too quickly and that, therefore, a return to the past is appropriate. Those who identify with the conservative part of the political spectrum are most frequently attracted to resistance movements. Members of the John Birch Society, for example, would be expected to find resistance movements attractive.

Reform movements are more likley to draw support from the politically moderate and liberal sections of the population. They attempt to progessively change some parts of the society that seem to be unjust or in a generally unsatisfactory condition. Job discrimination against physically handicapped veterans, for example, might stimulate the formation of a group to lobby for legislation which would solve this specific problem. **Revolutionary movements** sometimes scoff at reform attempts as patchwork done on an overall structure that is not worth saving. Radicals of the left, frequent participants in revolutionary movements, generally call for essential change of the whole system and the entire culture.

Few periods in twentieth-century America have seen as much social movement activity as the 1960s. Prominent among the movements were the anti-war movement, the civil rights movement, the women's liberation movement, and the ecology movement. Virtually no major institution in society went unchallenged. The movements just cited made struggle in political and economic institutions a frequent reality. The student power movement questioned the educational institution. The religious institution felt the impact of the "underground church" movement. The women's liberation movement called into question the female and male roles assigned to people in the family institution. Indeed, there was so much social movement activity in the 1960s that some referred to the existence of an overall "Movement" that was challenging America to move forward with progressive change. There are two relevant points to be made here. First, the 1960s movements showed a considerable amount of overlap in their memberships. Many anti-war activists, for example, were also involved in the attempt to win student power. A significant number of women involved in the cause of liberation were also active in other movements such as the ecology movement. These examples of overlap support the notion of an overall "Movement." Secondly, the idea that the individual movements fought for progressive change is supported by the fact that they generally had both reform and revolutionary strains within them. The civil rights movement, for example, had within it reform groups such as the NAACP and more revolutionary factions such as the Black Panthers. These different segments often disagreed with one another on a number of tactical issues, but they shared a general consensus on the goal of moving away from the mistreatment and neglect of blacks by American society.

While the 1960s did not have a social movement which directly challenged the concentration of wealth and power in upper-class America, a variety of movements fought this concentration indirectly. The poor people's movement called for a better economic situation for the bottom part of the non-upper class. The civil rights movement, through its efforts at improving the position of blacks in American society, effected a minor redistribution of power to some non-upper class people. The anti-war movement did combat with the military-industrial complex, a key source of upper-class wealth and power. Still, even in this time of activism, the power and wealth of the upper class were never directly challenged by a broad coalition of class-conscious non-upper class groups.

The 1970s, of course, present us with another story entirely. For a variety of reasons there has been less activism during the time now known as the "me decade."* Instead of directly attempting to alter social structures, the 1970s mentality has been one of egocentricity as evidenced by the interest in such things as est, TM, and religious cults. Nevertheless, there has been a number of social movements in the 1970s.

By way of comparison with the 1960s, the more recent movements have tended to be narrower in their focus and, for support, have drawn far more heavily from the politically

---

*The "me decade" is well reflected by the 1972 inaugural statement of Nixon: "In our own lives, let each of us ask, not just what will government do for me, but what can I do for myself." This was an interesting modification of the 1960 Kennedy inaugural statement, "Ask not what your country can do for you. Ask what you can do for your country."

moderate and conservative sections of the population. This is especially true with respect to the anti-busing and anti-abortion movements, generally classified as resistance movements because they represent backlash against changes initiated in the recent past. More difficult to classify is the anti-nuclear movement of the 1970s. A considerable number of liberals and radicals are involved in this movement, but also included are a substantial number of moderates and conservatives. Are we to call this a resistance movement against modern man's reliance upon advanced technology? Or, is this movement also influenced by reform and revolutionary motives of a progressive nature? All of these elements are very likely present.

The social movement activity of the 1970s will be discussed again later on in this chapter, but for now the following comments are in order. Virtually no one claims that an overall "Movement" existed during this period. This illustrates the smaller degree of movement activity in the 1970s. Also, as was the case with the 1960s, there has been some activity in the 1970s related to the class issue; but, once again, the relation has tended to be more indirect than direct.

CLASS RELATED ISSUES AND SOLUTIONS

Let us look closely at some of the issues and questions before the American people which bear directly and indirectly upon the problem of the concentration of power and wealth in America. We will begin by considering some of the ones indirectly related to altering the stratification situation with an eye on how they have not as yet generated a coalition of non-upper class people.

As already noted in Chapter 4, upper-class and white-collar Americans are highly concentrated in suburbia, whereas the blue-collar and poor are most frequently found in the central city. This residential separation by stratification groups is the result of, and reinforces, the relative economic and political advantage of the suburban groups. For example, because local property taxes are a major basis for supporting public education, suburbanites can create better schooling for their children than central city residents. This is due to the better economic position of those who live in suburbia. Also, suburbanites who work in the central city do not have to pay city taxes but do benefit from the city. For example, commuting suburbanites and the businesses that they work for in the city benefit by a host of city services such as the fire and police departments. Furthermore, suburbanites can fend off incursions by blue-collar and poor people into suburbia by snob housing ordinances. As an example, some suburban communities require that any new houses must be built on a large piece of property, for example, an acre of land. This automatically excludes the poor and blue-collar individuals from moving to suburbia. Finally, there is a lack of political connection and interaction between the central city and the suburbs. This enables suburbanites to maintain their advantages all the more readily because they are not as accountable for their advantages as they would be if more governmentally connected with the central city.

An interesting thing happens with regard to potential solutions for the suburban/central city division and its consequent disparities. For the most part, an alliance is formed between upper-class suburbanites and white-collar suburbanites against blue-collar and poor central city residents. As a result, the non-upper class is politically fractured. Examples of this abound. Metropolitan government and annexation, as means of dealing with the lack of political connection between the central city and suburbia, find a substantial lack of approval among both upper-class and white-collar suburbanites. So do proposals for a commuter tax or an anti-snob housing ordinance. Even when the latter is passed, implementation is resisted or the least threatening blue-collar or poor people, such as elderly whites, are encouraged to take advantage of the low and moderate priced housing that is created. Finally, proposals to do something about the unequal educational opportunity of central city students are not supported when they will chip away at the suburban advantage. An example is the effort to disconnect the local property tax from the support of public education. In its place, there could be a more equitable generalized pool funded by property taxes but distributed to communities on the basis of need. Both upper-class and white-collar suburbanites resist such proposals; moreover, their alliance divides the non-upper class within and against itself.

Another way in which the same phenomenon of non-upper class division occurs becomes apparent when one takes into consideration that central city/suburban residential separation also exists along racial lines. Central cities are disproportionately black, and suburbs are often virtually all white. A solution offered to deal with the black/white division has a bearing upon stratification alliances. Busing has been used for the purpose of attempting to achieve racial integration in the public schools. The way in which this has been implemented, however, restricts it to within the boundaries of the central city. Suburban school systems have not been included. Its net effect has been to pit poor blacks and blue-collar whites against each other in a fight over inadequate central city schooling that does not begin to compare with suburban schooling. Of course, if busing were to be broadened to include not only the central city but also suburbia, the result would begin a move toward both racial integration and class integration. Resistance to this proposal comes from the suburban world of both the upper-class and the white-collar worker. Once again, the white-collar population teams up with the upper class against segments of the non-upper class. Consequently, the non-upper class is politically divided.

MORE ISSUES AND SOLUTIONS

If a serious challenge is to be made against the concentration of power and wealth in the hands of the upper class, non-upper class America needs to be unified. Are there issues and solutions around which such unification can be effected? In fact, there is a broad range of issues around which the non-upper class can indeed come together. But crucial is how these issues and solutions are articulated. Are they framed in such a way that they benefit a large percentage of the non-upper class rather than dividing it up as the solutions discussed above tend to do? With this guiding question in mind, let us list some of these solutions to the problem of concentrated power and wealth and then consider the articulation of some of them in detail.

Among the most direct solutions to the concentration of wealth and power are: 1) tax reform, including the closing of upper-class tax loopholes; 2) placing a ceiling on the amount of income that can be earned by anyone; 3) reforming the financing of political campaigns; and 4) challenging the upper-class owned big businesses which control the economy. (A mild example of the latter would be to actually enforce antitrust legislation already on the books; whereas a more substantial illustration would be to push for the public ownership and democratic control of key industries in the economy.) Other solutions that are somewhat more indirectly related to attacking the upper-class domination of America, but that could potentially unify the non-upper class, are efforts that push for full employment; control of the inflation that eats away at non-upper class paychecks; a guaranteed annual income or a negative income tax plan; proper use of the environment; worker safety provisions; worker control of the workplace; and improvements in the overall systems of food production, education, health care, housing, transportation, and energy.

Are there any signs that non-upper class America is upset enough about upper-class domination of America to actually do something about it? Surprisingly enough, even in the middle of the "me decade," there are such signs. For example, Harris Poll data collected in 1966 and 1974 showed the following percentages of Americans expressing confidence in the following branches of the power elite as described by C. Wright Mills.

	1966	*1974*	*% Decline*
Major Companies	55	21	34
Executive Branch of Federal Government	41	28	13
The Military	62	32	30

Congress, another government sector highly influenced by the upper class, showed a similar decline from 42 percent in 1966 to 18 percent in 1974. These data reveal to some extent, no doubt, the effects of Viet Nam, Watergate, and the tighter economic situation of the early 1970s. But it can also be argued that they reveal considerable negative feelings about the upper class per se. Let us look at the issue of tax reform in this context. There is no question that President Carter based part of his 1976 campaign for election on the negative feelings that non-upper class people have towards the upper class. His assessment that the tax system was "a disgrace to the human race" left little doubt in this regard. Unfortunately, during his term in office very little was done to alter the tax situation at the federal level.

The current system of tax loopholes is easy to criticize from the standpoint of unfair upper-class advantage. The fact that J. Paul Getty and Richard Nixon paid the same amount of taxes yearly as someone with less than the median income shows this clearly. On the other hand, it is difficult to propose a system of taxation that corrects this problem and also convinces non-upper class people to give up the benefits that they receive from the current tax law. It is true, for example, that the family that earns a million dollars or more in yearly income benefits from the loopholes to the tune of $720,000, while the family with an income of $3,000 a year or less only gets a break of $16. But the same system also gives the family with an income in the twenty thousand to twenty-five thousand range a bonanza of $1,900. Is that family willing to give up its advantage in order to bring the upper class into line? The existing tax law, as illustrated by these loophole savings, is a classic example of legislation framed so that the upper class and part of the non-upper class are allied against the rest of the non-upper class. If the concentration of power and wealth are to be attacked, legislation that unites the non-upper class is needed.

California's Proposition 13 is another example of how the non-upper class can be divided against itself. The legislation was heralded for giving property tax relief to blue-collar and white-collar homeowners. The relief amounted to two billion dollars in the first year of its application. There are tradeoffs, of course. Even more tax relief was given to the upper-class dominated business community during the first year—three billion dollars. Also, basic public services have had to be cut back and will have to be cut back in the future. Part of the public services to be threatened is the welfare benefits for the poor. Through Proposition 13 the upper class, and a significant part of the non-upper class, have been united against the bottom part of the non-upper class. This alliance is in keeping with the tendency outlined in Chapters 3 and 4 to blame the poor and not to blame the upper class. It should be pointed out that services affecting white-collar and blue-collar people—schools, libraries, recreational facilities, police forces, and fire departments—are likely to be cut back more severely when the real crunch hits in California. A state budget surplus of 5 billion dollars enabled California to avoid some of this potential disaster during the first year of the new law's implementation. Similar moves to Proposition 13 have occurred in other states across the country since 1978. In fact, it is legitimate to speak of a taxpayer's revolt that has the shape of a social movement. In order for this movement seriously to challenge upper-class rule of America, however, its proposals need to be articulated in the manner that we have suggested—pro-non-upper class and anti-upper-class wealth and power—and, as we have suggested, it is possible to do so.

Any full-fledged movement of the non-upper class could and should involve other direct proposals to remedy the existing concentration of wealth and power in America. As many have indicated, a key change to fight for here is reform of the financing of political campaigns. This is critical if the upper class is to be prevented from merely buying politicians and consequently legislating their interests. As a response to Watergate, some laws have been passed which remove the possibility of a few rich people buying presidential candidates lock, stock, and barrel. In particular, they placed a limit on how much money an individual can contribute to a presidential candidate's campaign. Also, public financing of presidential campaigns was introduced. Even with these changes, however, special interests, many of which represented the upper class, contributed to the campaigns of both presidential candidates in 1976, so the population at large still had a choice between two candidates who were significantly influenced by the upper class. Therefore, tightening up of this legislation is needed. There is even a greater need for similar legislation regarding the public financing of federal congressional elections. Such legislation still did not exist for the 1980 elections. If appropriate changes in the financing of congressional elections do become a reality, it will be more likely that other direct challenges of the upper class can be made, such as non-upper class tax reform. Upper-class control of the economy through its virtual monopolies could be fought more effectively. Appointments to agencies that are supposed to regulate business would more likely be filled by people representing the public interest. The long range goal of public ownership of key industries—such as the energy related ones—would become more of a possibility.

Another way to alter the current stratification reality in America is to place a ceiling on income. This means, in effect, that no one would be allowed to earn above a certain level of income (possibly $100,000 a year, for example). This would have the effect of bringing the top part of the stratification system down. A way of implementing the ceiling concept would be to place a 100 percent tax on all income earned above $100,000 or some other cutoff point. Curiously enough, this is probably one of the proposals least likely to be favored by the non-upper class. To similar proposals made in the past, there has been deep opposition on the part of people from very humble financial backgrounds who have very little chance of earning anywhere near the maximum income allowed by the plans. A major reason for this opposition has been that many people who have no hope of making a large salary themselves still hold out that hope for their children. This does not mean that consideration of the ceiling on income proposal as a potential measure should be discarded. Like the public ownership of key industries, this proposal might begin to make more political sense as a viable non-upper class movement gained momentum and started to have an impact upon the American Dream Package part of the overall culture.

A few words about some of the indirect solutions to the concentration of wealth and power listed above are in order. Efforts to create full employment and control inflation do not directly attack upper-class wealth and power. They could do this indirectly, however, if they were designed so that their implementation cut into the upper class and not parts of the non-upper class. Pro-ecology proposals, for example, could challenge upper-class profits rather than non-upper class jobs. Such a strategy regarding indirect solutions to the concentration of power and wealth may sound harsh. However, it should be remembered that the problem which these solutions are aimed at exist in the first place because the upper class chooses its profits over non-upper class interests in a decent quality of life—one in which good food, air, water, health care, housing, education, transportation, and working conditions are within the grasp of all.

Given the attention it receives, some discussion of the guaranteed annual income as an indirect solution for the concentration of wealth and power is needed. This proposal would set a financial ground floor beneath which no family would be allowed to fall. As the ceiling on income proposal brings the top of the stratification system down, the guaranteed annual income plan brings the bottom part of the stratification system up. Ideally, the floor would be set at a level high enough to insure that all Americans could afford the basic necessities of life: adequate food, clothing, and shelter.* Some non-upper class people react to this proposal negatively because they think that they will be supporting the poor with their tax money: "It's my tax dollars that will pay for this." "Why should I work to support people who will get a free ride?" Once again, the message is clear. Proposals have to be made in such a way that they do not divide the non-upper class. A guaranteed annual income proposal, for instance, could include a sliding scale which encourages people to work rather than not work. It will also be helpful if this proposal is part of an overall agenda of proposals that together benefits the entire non-upper class.

NATURE OF PROPOSED SOCIAL CLASS MOVEMENT

If a movement based on the issues and solutions listed above were to develop, what kind of social movement would it be? It is, of course, somewhat presumptuous to speculate on this. One's first inclination is to suspect that it would most likely be either a reform movement, a revolutionary movement, or a combination of the two. The possibility of a combination calls

---

*Congress has considered bills sponsoring guaranteed annual income approaches. Usually, the bills set the financial ground floor at a level considerably less than the poverty level. None, however, has passed both the Senate and the House of Representatives as of this date.

to mind Slater's (1976:134) suggestion that both liberal and radical elements have to be strong if meaningful social change is to take place. The two elements cannot be out to destroy each other, as was sometimes the case in movements of the 1960s, if real change is to occur. In fact, these elements have their respective roles to play. Liberal elements supporting reforms that alleviate problems in the short run are to be encouraged because they improve the lives of non-upper class people. Such reforms do not have to lead to the co-optation of movement energy and goals. Indeed, they can raise expectations of even more basic systemic changes needed in the political and economic organization of the society. Hence, liberal reforms can prepare the way and the need for more radical change.

Assuming that an alliance of reform and revolutionary factions could be developed, would this mean that the resistance and conservative parts of the political spectrum would be excluded? Not necessarily, by any means. It is possible that a movement based upon the attempt to break up the upper-class concentration of wealth and power could be articulated and perceived as attractive by a significant number of conservative people. For one thing, successful efforts to diminish upper-class power would mean a return to a situation where power was not as concentrated at the top—to a time when political democracy was more in evidence. Furthermore, successful attacks on upper-class wealth and its basis, the large corporations, would ultimately mean an improvement in the economic situation of the "little guy," currently excluded from the possibility of competing with the corporate giants. In the final analysis, it is feasible to develop a social movement aimed at challenging the upper class wealth and power which has appeal to the full range of political ideologies. Indeed, in all likelihood it will be necessary to do so if such a movement is to have a reasonable chance of success.

CAUTIONS

There are a number of concerns that any movement for change along the lines suggested here should be prepared for. As just indicated, it is desirable to have a broad base of support. Different parts of the political spectrum should not be automatically ruled out, and different parts of the non-upper class should not be excluded. Both the language and the tone of appeals made by those who develop the movement are critical. The message presented should be loud and clear; but the tone should not be so strident that it turns people off. There are numerous examples of this point. Some parts of the "Movement" during the 1960s adopted a deliberately "freaky" style—the "Yippies," for example—which had the effect of alienating people who might otherwise have been sympathetic. Even when a "non-straight" demeanor is not deliberately adopted, opposition forces will search out some such evidence, or create it, in order to label a group's efforts negatively and therefore discredit them. An example of an attempt to create such evidence is one of the "dirty tricks" attributed to the 1972 Nixon re-election campaign where a group of blatant homosexuals was allegedly paid to march in front of the McGovern campaign headquarters and declare that they were "for George." The strategy of negative labeling and the hope for fall-out from McGovern support were obvious here.

Another aspect of the problem of language and tone needs mention. Efforts to challenge upper-class wealth and power often have been fought by suggesting that they are "socialistic" which, in turn, becomes equated with "communistic." The role of the negative associations with communism (atheism, loss of freedom, and overthrow of government) in making people afraid of social movements hardly needs to be mentioned.* With this in mind, it is advisable for proponents of egalitarian change to choose wisely the language describing their proposals For example, it would seem wise to use the word *democratization* to describe the overall process called for by the direct and indirect solutions mentioned in our previous discussion. Closing the tax loopholes, for instance, and even public ownership of

---

*An interesting point here is that when upper-class people and institutions make moves capable of being interpreted as friendly to socialism, the communist threat is not brought up very much. When Chase Manhattan Bank opened up its Moscow branch office at 1 Karl Marx Place, it went relatively unnoticed on the financial pages of the newspaper.

key industries would mean that America was moving in the direction of making the economy democratic. After all, democracy is one of the things that America stands for.

A further cautionary note relates to the possibility of repression. If the recent past is any barometer, one can conceive that the class movement suggested here would face such difficulties. It is now known, for example, that the FBI engaged in acts of blackmail, burglary, and violence in order to thwart people active in the social movements of the 1960s. Such harassment was also aimed at "neutralizing" leaders of movements. Thus, it is still the case that there is strong suspicion of FBI involvement in the assassinations of Martin Luther King and Fred Hampton, a Black Panther leader in Chicago. Obviously, social movement activity on the part of the non-upper class always carries with it the possibility of attempts at repression. This does not mean that there should not be a social movement to challenge upper-class wealth and power. It does mean that precautions should be taken.

A very important question that a class movement would have to deal with relates to "victories." Assuming that the movement was somewhat successful, each victory would have to be analyzed from the standpoint of whether or not real change was accomplished or merely palliatives were created. An example of the latter is presented by Domhoff (1970) who suggests that the labor movement in the US was headed off by a liberal faction of the upper class. This was accomplished when modest reforms such as Social Security were backed by part of the upper class with the hope that if the reforms were made, more serious demands by the non-upper class would be silenced and eliminated. The strategy worked.

There is a further point about "victories." Movements involving non-upper class people who must work nine to five every day have to struggle to get significant involvement by movement members. It is problematic enough to organize activity for a big event—a march on Washington, for example. Sustained activity is even more difficult to achieve; yet it is needed if real victories are to be won and maintained. Sometimes minor concessions are granted after a big demonstration that are later revoked when everyone returns to work. After a large demonstration at Seabrook, New Hampshire, in 1978, for example, the decision was made to halt construction of the nuclear site. Shortly thereafter, once everyone was involved in their daily routines, construction was resumed. Those behind a non-upper class movement must be aware of similar possibilities because the upper class, especially through its corporate lobbyists in Washington, is able to carry on a daily battle to preserve its position. Tuckman (1973) calls this battle a "war for wealth." The social movement that we are suggesting would have to fight unceasingly, too. As a start, more non-upper class lobbyists, "people lobbyists," are needed in Washington and in the state capitals throughout the country.

What should be the preeminent concern of those interested in developing the proposed non-upper class movement is the difficulty in getting a broad coalition of non-upper class people together. As Chapter 3 indicates, the American culture is very pro-upper class. This means that a significant number of white-collar, blue-collar, and poor people behave in ways that ultimately suit the interests of the upper class. Goertzel (1976), among others, points out how the upper class has been successful in getting a significant number of blue-collar people to point the finger of blame down, at the poor, rather than up, at the upper class. This problem also exists in the white-collar world. Rossides (1976:468-469), for example, suggests that the upper class and the upper levels of the white-collar world form a basic alliance and run the country. Similarly, it can be argued that because people from the top of the white-collar world can afford a comfortable life-style (Happy American Suburban Home Ownership), they are unlikely to support any effort at changing economic stratification in America. They have been co-opted. While some of this is true, it would still seem to be in the best interests of the top part of the white-collar world to support many of the solutions to the upper class concentration of wealth and power listed previously.

Even if all of the upper-level, white-collar people went over to the side of the upper class, it would still leave about 85 percent of the population as potential support for a non-upper class movement. However, the pro-upper class bias in the culture might well divide the remaining members of the non-upper class, as it could encourage some to ally with the upper class. Still, the position of this book is that the basic stratification split in America positions the upper class against the non-upper class. Nevertheless, it seems that when the upper class allows the white-collar world to enter into a coalition with it against the rest of the stratification system (the blue-collar and poor), a substantial part of the white-collar world is more than willing to do so. Witness the alliances formed in response to the potential solutions to the suburban/central city division discussed earlier in this chapter. When the upper class invites both the white-collar and blue-collar worlds into a coalition against the poor, this may also happen because of the tendency of many to identify up and blame down. All of this must eventually be changed if the non-upper class is to alter its situation.

MOVEMENT PROSPECTS

The direct and indirect solutions discussed earlier can form a working agenda for a non-upper class movement: They further the goal of democratizing the economic and political institutions. Is there any sign of such a movement now as the 1980s start? Yes. The beginnings of a non-upper class movement can be seen in a variety of national, state, and local groups. National groups such as Common Cause have already been effective in the area of reforming the rules affecting political campaigns. State groups, such as the public interest research groups encouraged by Ralph Nader, have challenged the concentration of power and wealth through a broad range of consumer-oriented issues. Groups on the neighborhood level have become concerned with the ill effects of big government and big business on their communities. All of these groups work for many of the potential solutions to the concentration of wealth and power.

A variety of specialized groups also push for relevant change. Some groups focus on taxation. Massachusetts Fair Share, for example, works for tax reform, often with special emphasis placed upon the tax loopholes that benefit the upper class. A number of unions regularly fight for better wages and working conditions for large numbers of workers; they also support proposals that benefit the wider non-upper class population such as guaranteed annual income proposals. The Gray Panthers, an organization concerned with the problems of the elderly, suggest that their problems are significantly related to the concentration of wealth and power at the top of the society. Ecology groups struggle for the proper use of the environment and often challenge upper-class dominated businesses. Anti-nuclear groups such as Clamshell Alliance and Mobilization for Survival threaten a source of upper-class wealth when they fight for solar energy. (The large corporations are less likely to make huge profits if the sun becomes a major energy source since the corporations have not figured out a way to take possession of the sun.) One can point to other rays of hope, such as certain women's organizations, a variety of communal life styles, and some religious groups which are attuned to non-upper class issues and positions. The list could go on and on. Importantly, these trends are not just on the liberal and radical sides of the political spectrum. Some moderate and conservative politicians recently have been calling for the public ownership of the oil industry in these days of oil shortage.

All of these trends challenge upper-class power and wealth. What is needed, of course, is their expansion and elaboration. The obstacles to a non-upper class movement must be dealt with, however, if this is to materialize. For example, there is potential for the development of tax reform as a non-upper class issue. If this is to happen, though, the alliances between the upper class and the non-upper class must be challenged and broken. In general, the people in the middle of America, a large section of the non-upper class, do feel squeezed economically but direct their anger at the poor rather than at the rich. If a successful non-upper class movement is to become a reality, then this non-upper class split—as well as others caused by race, religion, nationality, residence, sex, and status—must be dealt with. Even more broadly, the institutions and cultural beliefs which perpetuate upper-class domination of America must be successfully challenged. And, of course, the non-upper class must become more conscious of its true position vis à vis the upper class and develop political unity and strength based upon this consciousness.

But the concentration of wealth and power outlined in Chapter 2 is so devastating that it is easy for many non-upper class people to become discouraged and sometimes apathetic. "What can I do against the trends of wealth and power concentration which seem so permanent and strong?" Actually, as indicated, a number of confrontations with the trends of concentration have been taking place. In fact, upper-class domination would probably be much worse today had such confrontations not occurred. The point is that more of this activity needs to be formed, discovered, and joined because the slogan of the 1960s still has relevance: "If you're not part of the solution, then you're part of the problem."

What are the chances of a full-fledged, non-upper class movement developing in the near future? It's hard to speak definitely, but some trends are discernible. If we look at the 1970s, we find both good and bad news. The good news is the movement activity that revolves around the concentration of wealth and power. The bad news is that overall the 1970s have been a time of considerably less movement activity than the 1960s. This is the "me decade" part of the story. On a more positive note, a number of people see a return to social movement activity in the 1980s. Historian Arthur Schlesinger assesses the situation in the following way:

> In the 1960s we had the civil rights revolution, the war in Vietnam which no one understood, the turbulence on the campuses, the alienation of the young, and then Watergate. That left the nation exhausted. In a certain sense the 70s are like the 50s and 20s—a period when sights are lowered and no one wants to do anything. But these periods never last because when no one does anything, problems begin to accumulate, and pretty soon the dam will break. The 1980s will be a period of movement, like the 60s and the 30s (Boston Sunday Globe, 1978:3).

The coming movement activity should be aimed at combating and removing the inequality in America caused by the concentration of wealth and power in the hands of the upper class.

REFERENCES

Anderson, Charles
    1974   *The Political Economy of Social Class.* Englewood Cliffs, New Jersey: Prentice-Hall.

Anderson, Charles and Jeffrey Gibson
    1978   *Toward a New Sociology.* Homewood, Illinois: Dorsey Press.

Anderson, Jack and Les Whitten
    1977   "Big Oil Lobbyists Maintain Strong Influence." *Boston Evening Globe,* April 22, p. 23

Aronowitz, Stanley
    1973   *False Promises.* New York: McGraw-Hill.

Baker, Russell
    1977   "A Taxpayer's Prayer." *New York Times,* April 10, Section 6, p. 12.

Baltzell, E. Digby
    1958   *Philadelphia Gentlemen.* Glencoe, Illinois: Free Press.

Berle, Adolph and Gardiner Means
    1967   *The Modern Corporation and Private Property.* New York: Harcourt, Brace and World.

Blau, Peter and Otis D. Duncan
    1967   *The American Occupational Structure.* New York: Wiley.

Boston Sunday Globe
    1978   "Arthur Schlesinger Answers His Critics." October 1, Section A. p. 3.

Bowles, Samuel and Herbert Gintis
    1976   *Schooling in Capitalist America.* New York: Basic Books.

Braverman, Harry
  1974   *Labor and Monopoly Capital.* New York: Monthly Review Press.
Breecher, Jeremy
  1978   "Uncovering the Hidden History of the American Workplace."
          Review of Radical Political Economics 10:1-23.
Breslin, Jimmy
  1973   *World Without End, Amen.* New York: Viking Press.

————.

  1975   "A City Gasps for Its Life." *Boston Globe,* August 22, p. 23.
Carchedi, Guglielmo
  1977   *On the Economic Identification of Social Classes.* London:
          Routledge and Kegan Paul.
Centers, Richard
  1949   *The Psychology of Social Classes.* Princeton: Princeton Univer-
          sity Press.
Chinoy, Ely
  1955   *Automobile Workers and the American Dream.* New York:
          Random House.
Cohen, Albert and Harold Hodges
  1963   "Lower-Blue Collar Characteristics." *Social Problems* 10:
          303-334.
Coles, Robert
  1977   *Privileged Ones.* Boston: Little, Brown.
Dahl, Robert
  1961   *Who Governs?* New Haven: Yale University Press.
Davis, Kingsley and Wilbert Moore
  1945   "Some Principles of Stratification." *American Sociological
          Review* 10:242-249.
Domhoff, G. William
  1967   *Who Rules America?* Englewood Cliffs, New Jersy: Prentice-
          Hall.

————.

  1970   *The Higher Circles.* New York: Random House.

————.

  1972   *Fat Cats and Democrats.* Englewood Cliffs, New Jersey:
          Prentice-Hall.

Durkeim, Emile
1948   *The Elementary Forms of Religious Life,* trans. Joseph Ward Swain. New York: Free Press.

Feldman, Arnold and Charles Tilly
1960   "The Interaction of Social and Physical Space." *American Sociological Review* 25:877-884.

Forbes
1977   "Who Gets the Most Pay?" May 15, pp. 244-284.

Glock, Charles and Rodney Stark
1965   *Religion and Society in Tension.* Chicago: Rand-McNally.

Goertzel, Ted
1976   *Political Society.* Chicago: Rand-McNally.

Goodwin, Leonard
1972   *Do the Poor Want to Work?* Washington, D.C.: Brookings Institution.

Gordon, Milton
1963   *Social Class in American Sociology.* New York: McGraw-Hill.

Heilbroner, Robert
1965   *The Limits of American Capitalism.* New York: Harper and Row.

Heller, Joseph
1974   *Something Happened.* New York: Alfred A. Knoff.

Herberg, Will
1955   *Protestant, Catholic, and Jew.* Garden City, New York: Doubleday.

Hill, Gladwin
1970   "Polluters Sit on Antipollution Boards." *New York Times,* December 7, p. 1.

Hodge, R. W., P. M. Siegal, and P. H. Rossi
1964   "Occupational Prestige in the United States, 1925-1963." *American Journal of Sociology* 70:286-302.

Hoffman, William
1971   *David.* New York: Lyle Stuart.

Hollingshead, August
1949   *Elmtown's Youth.* New York: Wiley.

Hunter, Floyd
 1953   *Community Power Structure.* Chapel Hill: University of North Carolina Press.

Internal Revenue Service
 1978   *Statistics of Income – 1975, Individual Income Tax Returns.* Washington, D.C.

Jencks, Christopher et al.
 1972   *Inequality: A Reassessment of the Effect of Family and Schooling in America.* New York: Basic Books.

Karabel, Jerome
 1972   "Community Colleges and Social Stratification." *Harvard Educational Review* 42:521-562.

————.
 1979   "The Reasons Why." *The New York Review of Books* 26:22-27.

Komarovsky, Mirra
 1964   *Blue-Collar Marriage.* New York: Random House.

Laumann, Edward
 1966   *Prestige Association in an Urban Community.* New York: Bobbs-Merill.

Le Masters, E. E.
 1975   *Blue Collar Aristocrats.* Madison: University of Wisconsin Press.

Lenski, Gerhard
 1966   *Power and Privilege.* New York: McGraw-Hill.

Levison, Andrew
 1974   *The Working-Class Majority.* New York: Penguin Books.

Levitan, Sar
 1977   "War on Poverty Ended, but Poverty Didn't." *Boston Globe,* August 11, p. 18.

Lewis, Michael
 1978   *The Culture of Inequality.* Amherst: University of Massachusetts Press.

Liebow, Elliot
 1967   *Tally's Corner.* Boston: Little, Brown.

Lundberg, Ferdinand
 1968   *The Rich and the Super-Rich.* New York: Lyle Stuart.

Lynd, Robert and Helen Lynd
 1929   *Middletown.* New York: Harcourt, Brace and Company.

———.
1937   *Middletown in Transition.* New York: Harcourt, Brace and Company.

Lyons, Richard
1978   "Gifts from Parents to 'Buy' Places in Professional Schools on the Rise." *New York Times,* April 23, p. 1.

Marx, Gary
1967   *Protest and Prejudice.* New York: Harper and Row.

Marx, Karl
1948   *The Communist Manifesto.* New York: International Publishers.

———.
1967   *Capital.* New York: International Publishers.

Miliband, Ralph
1977   *Marxism and Politics.* Oxford: Oxford University Press.

Mills, C. Wright
1951   *White Collar.* New York: Oxford University Press.

———.
1956   *The Power Elite.* New York: Oxford University Press.

Miller, Judith
1978   "Interlocking Directorates Flourish." *New York Times,* Section 3, p. 2.

Nader, Ralph and Mark Green
1973   "Owing Your Soul to the Company Store." *The New York Review of Books* 20:37-42.

North, C. C. and P. K. Hatt
1947   "Jobs and Occupations: A Popular Evaluation." *Opinion News* 9:3-13.

Page, Charles
1969   *Class and American Sociology: From Ward to Ross.* New York: Schocken Books.

Park, Robert
1926   "The Urban Community as a Spacial Pattern and a Moral Order," in *The Urban Community,* ed., Ernest Burgess. Chicago: The University of Chicago Press.

Parkin, Frank
1971   *Class Inequality and Political Order.* New York: Praeger.

Piven, Francis Fox and Richard Cloward
1971   *Regulating the Poor.* New York: Random House.

Poulantzas, Nicos
1975   *Classes in Contemporary Capitalism.* London: New Left Books.

Projector, Dorothy and Gertrude Weiss
1966   *Survey of Financial Characteristics of Consumers.* Washington, D.C.: Federal Reserve Board.

Ravitch, Diane
1978   *The Revisionists Revisited.* New York: Basic Books.

Reissman, Leonard
1959   *Class in American Society.* Glencoe, Illinois: Free Press.

————.
1973   *Inequality in American Society.* Glenview, Illinois: Scott, Foresman and Company.

Rist, R. C.
1970   "Student Social Class and Teacher's Expectations: The Self-fulfilling Prophecy in Ghetto Education." *Harvard Educational Review* 40:411-450.

Roach, Jack, Llewellyn Gross, and Orville Gursslin
1969   *Social Stratification in the United States.* Englewood Cliffs, New Jersey: Prentice-Hall.

Rosenthal, Robert and Lenore Jacobson
1968   *Pygmalion in the Classroom.* New York: Holt, Rinehart and Winston.

Rossides, Daniel
1976   *The American Class System.* Boston: Houghton Mifflin.

Roszak, Theodore
1969   *The Making of a Counterculture.* Garden City, New York: Doubleday.

Ryan, William
1976   *Blaming the Victim.* New York: Random House.

Rytina, Joan, William Form, and John Pease
1970   "Income and Stratification Ideology: Beliefs about the American Opportunity Structure." *American Journal of Sociology* 75:702-716.

Sale, Kilpatrick
1975   *Power Shift.* New York: Random House.

Sennett, Richard and Jonathan Cobb
1972   *The Hidden Injuries of Class.* New York: Random House.

Sewell, William and Vimal Shah
1967   "Socioeconomic Status, Intelligence, and the Attainment of Higher Education." *Sociology of Education* 40:1-23.

Slater, Philip
1976   *The Pursuit of Loneliness.* Boston: Beacon Press.

_____.
1977   *Footholds.* New York: E. P. Dutton.

Smith, James
1974   "The Concentration of Personal Wealth in America, 1969." *Review of Income and Wealth* 20: 143-180.

Smith, James, Steven Franklin, and Douglas Wion
1974   "Distribution of Financial Assets," in *In the Pockets of a Few,* ed., Fred Harris. New York: Grossman.

Stack Carol
1975   *All Our Kin.* New York: Harper and Row.

Stern, Philip
1973   *The Rape of the Taxpayer.* New York: Random House.

Stouffer, Samuel
1955   *Communism, Conformity, and Civil Liberties.* Garden City. New York: Doubleday.

TRB
1976   "Tax Grabs." *Boston Globe,* July 10, p. 7.

Terkel, Studs
1974   *Working.* New York: Pantheon Books.

Thurow, Lester and Robert Lucas
1972   *The American Distribution of Income: A Structural Problem.* Washington, D.C.: Government Printing Office.

Tuckman, Howard
1973   *The Economics of the Rich.* New York: Random House.

Tully, J. C., E. F. Jackson, and R. F. Curtis
1970   "Trends in Occupational Mobility in Indianapolis." *Social Forces* 49:186-200.

Turner, Jonathan and Charles Starnes
1976   *Inequality: Privilege and Poverty in America.* Pacific Palisades. California: Goodyear Publishing Company.

U.S. Bureau of the Census
1974   *Social and Economic Characteristics of Students: October 1973,* Series P-20, No. 272. Washington, D.C.: Government Printing Office.

_____.

1976   *Statistical Abstract of the United States: 1976.* Washington, D.C.

_____.

1977   *Statistical Abstract of the United States: 1977.* Washington, D.C.

Vanfossen, Beth
1979   *The Structure of Social Inequality.* Boston: Little, Brown.

von Hoffman, Nicholas
1979   "The Solid Gold Cornflake." *The New York Review of Books* 26:21-23.

Walton, John
1966   "Substance and Artifact: The Current Status of Research on Community Power Structure." *American Journal of Sociology* 71:430-438.

Warner, W. Lloyd and Paul S. Lunt
1941   *The Social Life of a Modern Community.* New Haven: Yale University Press.

Warner, W. Lloyd et al.
1949   *Democracy in Jonesville.* New York: Harper and Row.

Warner, W. Lloyd with Marchia Meeker and Kenneth Eells
1960   *Social Class in America.* New York: Harper and Row.

Wattenberg, Ben
1974   *The Real America.* New York: G. P. Putnam's Sons.

Weber, Max
1946   *Max Weber: Essays in Sociology,* trans. H. H. Gerth and C. Wright Mills. New York: Oxford University Press.

Williams, Robin
1970   *American Society: A Sociological Interpretation.* New York: Alfred A. Knopf.

Wright, Charles and Herbert Hyman
1958   "Voluntary Association Membership Among American Adults: Evidence from National Sample Surveys." *American Sociological Review* 23:284-294.

Zeitlin, Maurice
1978   "Who Owns America?" *The Progressive* 42:14-19.